Priase for *Dilemma*

Retired Sergeant "Buz"   elf
as a serious author in th   )lt
the reader from the first p   ᵍ ₋₋ₚ₋₋ ₋₋ₗ₋ₒ a crime drama that
will capture your intrigue, heighten your interest, guide
you through the inner workings of a criminal mind, and
reveal what field police work can do, and finally leave you
with one more mystery that you, the reader, must resolve.

Sergeant Williams' three generations of law enforcement
comes into play to create an archetypical villain, "The
Skulker." There are times you might find sympathy in an
abused child's past but then you must question whether
evil can ever be forgiven for the malice it practices on its
unsuspecting victims. Unless you decided, as The Skulker
did that they deserved it.

Dilemma interweaves the suspense of a highly intelligent
criminal who seemingly has researched his evil trade
to deter detection and capture, and has an escape plan
for all possibilities to prevent his apprehension. Police
officers reading this will feel the familiar frustrations of
endeavoring to do their best to protect victims and get
justice for those wronged. While good police work is done
co-consciously, there is always the needed friend of luck to
break a case.

You will find in this novel too that all-important element
for police officers—to survive the evil they witness. Police
humor, sometimes called "gallows humor," macabre,
acerbic, but mostly hilarious, breaks the tensions between
reality and allows them to reassimilate into their families
and communities. I might also rerecommended Sergeant
Williams' first book, Police Pranks, Jokes, and Other
Stories Not Suitable For Children as a suitable transition

in knowledge to understanding this unique incongruous quality that causes amusement.

Finally, dear reader, I recommend to you this novel Dilemma for the entertainment and lingering suspense that will leave you reflecting, "Did I just read a confession or...."

—**John J. Garry,** Retired Police Sergeant, LBPD and Current Mayor for the City of Yerington, Nevada

In *Dilemma*, Buz Williams brings police drama to life in a manner that only a former cop can. With his decades of frontline police work, he's seen it all, from the hilarious to the heartbreaking—the stories and the characters in his book ring true. I highly recommend *Dilemma*.

—**Mike Rothmiller,** New York Times and International Bestselling Author and former detective.

DILEMMA

Buz Williams

Los Angeles, California, USA

Dilemma
Copyright © 2021 Richard Williams

This is a work of fiction. Any resemblance to real places, events, or persons living or dead is entirely coincidental.

Published by:
Genius Book Publishing
31858 Castaic Road, #154
Castaic, California 91384
GeniusBookPublishing.com

ISBN: 978-1-947521-70-4

211007 LH

PREFACE

You never find yourself until you face the truth
—Pearl Bailey

January 2005, Long Beach, California. After thirty years as a cop, I have seen a lot of changes. When I first joined the Long Beach Police Department in February 1975, it was a different city—a different time with a different people. Long Beach was no longer "Iowa by the Sea," as evidenced by the Pussycat Movie Theater on Ocean Boulevard, the Roxy porno theater on Pine, and all the sailor bars in the downtown area. The Pike, which was a pre-Disneyland amusement park on the beach, was on its last legs. The Navy Base and the Shipyard were both still going strong, thanks to the residuals of the Viet Nam War. Almost all of the once-resplendent hotels on Ocean Boulevard were, by the time

I graduated from the Academy, homes for seniors. In fact, there were so many retirees living in the city that one of my training officers referred to Long Beach as "the home of the newly wed and the nearly dead."

Most of the older people and business owners loved cops. The young adults, most of whom smoked a little dope now and then, tolerated us. Most of the college and high school students pretty much hated our guts. Even though we had several Black policemen, the large Black population treated us like an occupying army, and we pretty much acted like one. We had several women officers, but there was only one who worked the streets. The others worked juvenile or women's jail.

This is the side of the story you never hear. It's not pretty. It will piss off a lot of people. It will be denied. It will be scorned. It will be repudiated. It will cause all those reactions because it is God's Truth. I suppose, sometimes, "the truth will set you free." But, most times, the truth will rip your entrails out and kick you in the nuts for good measure. Most people can't stomach that, if you will pardon the pun. But one of the pleasant by-products of the First Amendment is that, on rare occasions, the Truth does see the light of day. When that happens, the pot gets stirred and someone might just see things as they really are—without any bullshit or what they now call "spin."

Anyhow, the first lesson I learned, after hitting the streets, was that there really are two sides to every story. This is how I had this lesson branded into my memory. My second training officer was Ron Helper. He had been on the PD for seven years, and had a reputation as a great street cop. Ron had answered the radio when the dispatcher called our unit, sending us on a neighborhood dispute call. (It was only my second month in a black & white, after the month before on graveyard patrol.) When we arrived at the complaining party's house, we were met by a sweet-looking woman named Mrs. Eldon, who was about 55. She told us that her next-door neighbor on the South had thrown a large paper grocery bag (they did not use plastic back then) full of dog poop (her word) over the fence into her backyard. She further told us it was not the first time this had happened. He had done this three or four times in the past, and she was getting sick and tired of it. She described him as a male, White, 25, 5'10", 190 pounds, brown hair, brown eyes, named Joe Caledra.

When this sweet, little lady had finished speaking, I was ready to go next door and knock this guy's "dick in the dirt" (a phrase I had heard for the first time on the graveyard shift the month before). As we were walking over there, I asked my partner, "What kind of an asshole would do such a thing to such a nice lady, Ron?" He just looked at me and said, "Well, let's just wait and see what he has to say." When Joe answered our knock, he was closer to 5'7" and weighed roughly 160 pounds. So much for eyewitness credibility.

Joe was friendly, cooperative, and admitted that he had indeed thrown the "bag of dog shit" (his word) over into his neighbor's yard. But, Joe claimed, he was merely returning his neighbor's property. It seemed that she had a habit of walking her large Lab/Great Dane mix every day. Every day, her dog would do his duty in Joe's yard, right under his pepper tree. For months, Joe had been asking, begging, and threatening his defiant neighbor not to let her dog defecate (my word) in his yard. After these numerous attempts at reason had been rebuffed, Joe decided to take matters into his own hands, so to speak.

My training officer and I walked Joe over to Mrs. Eldon's house. After some recriminations, Mrs. Eldon admitted that she did purposefully allow her dog to "poop" in Joe's yard, in retaliation for Joe purposefully turning his sprinklers on high to get her car wet and spotted. Joe (who admitted that he gathered some "extra dog and cat shit" from other neighbors' yards) stated that he only turned the sprinklers on high in a futile attempt to muddy his yard so Mrs. Eldon's dog would not "crap" there.

The point of this updated version of *The Gift of the Magi* is that you cannot usually find the truth with just one side of the story. Human nature being what it is, even if we think we are telling the absolute truth, we will always put our side of the story in the best light. Mrs. Eldon was not lying. She had just left out a fact or two that would not have made her look so good. Everybody does it to some degree. It's human nature.

Of course, police officers do the same thing. Regardless of what some obnoxious law professors/attorneys say about cops "testi-lying" (You can surely believe what lawyers say! That is why many of them call their J.D. degree a "license to steal."), lying is not taught in the Police Academy. As a matter of course, the opposite is taught, as it should be. When an individual is caught in a lie, his credibility is shot and can never be fully recovered. When a cop is caught in a highly publicized lie, the entire police profession's credibility is hurt in the public eye. Almost every police department will terminate a police officer who commits perjury, lies on reports, or manufactures evidence. Those dirty cops *should* be fired. They make the rest of us look bad and destroy the faith the public has in one of its institutions. But that is another story for another day.

The point to *this* story is that you can't find the truth without hearing all sides of an incident. Street cops know this. Detectives know it. Police brass should know it, though they seldom exhibit that knowledge. Police reporters know it… but, more often than not, fail to practice it in their stories because, they claim, deadlines do not allow for it. Most important of all, I know it. That is my dilemma. I know, love, admire, and respect the Truth. Yet, for the last few decades, I have been living with a lie. Not a little white lie, either. A big ugly, bold-faced, knee jarring, gut wrenching lie.

I executed a man. Well, not a man, really. Isn't that the way we rationalize? We dehumanize our enemies; it makes them easier to kill. I mean, in the Civil War, the South was not killing men, they were killing "Yankees." (As a Dodgers and Angels fan, I can understand that!) and the North was killing "Rebs." The fact remains that it is easier to kill someone you don't consider human or in any way like yourself. When you don't have to consider that the enemy soldier may have a wife or mother or children, it is a lot easier to pull the trigger or plunge the bayonet. Of course, the fact that the enemy soldier may be trying to do the same thing to you helps considerably to overcome any prior socialization *not to* "kill thy neighbor."

But the dehumanizing is not restricted to war or the military, it happens today in everyday life. Love may make the world go 'round, but hate really gets it spinning.

At any rate, my dilemma is not that I lied about the execution I performed. I never lied. It is not about me feeling guilty sending this predatory, homicidal, pusillanimous cocksucker to a premature meeting with his Maker. I don't. In fact, my *only* regret about dispatching this miserable prick into the next world is that he didn't suffer nearly enough prior to leaving this one. My only solace in this regard is that a good and just God will be French-frying the asshole's gonads for eternity. (By the way, you may think that my dehumanized description of my "victim" is a rationalization and makes me a hypocrite, but please withhold your judgment until you have read my whole story.) The dilemma is that, due to the circumstances, I was never given the opportunity to tell my side of the story. My conscience demands that I explain what happened, which I think is completely justifiable morally, but indefensible legally.

My feeling is that the vast majority of people who read this story will agree with that assessment. There will be those (the

ACLU, trial lawyers, bleeding hearts, and those suffering from alien abduction) who think that a dastardly crime has gone unpunished and will demand my head on a platter. However, I have grown accustomed to my head's current placement and wish to keep it exactly where it is, thank you very much.

The irony here is that I am trying to tell the Truth. That is something you will seldom get from your average Chief of Police in a lot of jurisdictions, nowadays. The reason is that most Chiefs of Police now are eunuchs. Back in the day, Chiefs had civil service protection. That enabled them to keep their testes where they belonged. If a mayor or city councilman ordered the Chief to do something stupid or corrupt, the Chief could tell them "no" and still keep his job. If one of the officers did something that looked bad to the media, and the politicians wanted to fire the officer, even though what he or she did was in policy and legal, that Chief could do the right thing, defend his officer, and suffer no career-ending consequences.

Today, however, most Chiefs of Police serve at the pleasure of the mayor, city manager, or a politically appointed police commission. If that Chief does not bow to the political and/or media pressure, he will be fired, or at least demoted. To me, that is a prescription for corruption, disaster, and spineless police chiefs.

To adequately explain my position and my reasoning that this unauthorized execution was morally justifiable, I must educate the reader as to how I came to the situation that led to this "death dance." To do that, I must first give my history and my philosophy in my area of expertise—law enforcement. I must take you, the reader, through my education as a rookie and maturing young cop and show you the funny side, the tragic side, and the frustrating side of modern police work.

I must say I am quite thankful I never made it past sergeant. I know the public perception is that lieutenants are the workhorses of a police department, but nothing could be further from the truth. In every movie and TV show you watch, the homicide detective is a lieutenant. What a crock. Lieutenants sit on their asses in offices. They take orders from captains, commanders, and deputy chiefs, and give orders to sergeants, corporals, detectives, and officers. They attend management training days, community meetings, neighborhood Watch meetings, and area meetings with the aides to city council members. The good lieutenants realize they make good money for a superfluous position, give their sergeants direction, and step out of the way while the sergeants and their teams get the job done.

In the Long Beach Police Department, we do not have captains. When I was first hired, we did have them. They had civil service protection and the city management thought that it was more important to promote ass kissing than competency. Similarly, with the chiefs of police before them, civil service gave captains the liberty of telling their superiors the truth about any given problem without fear of losing their job or rank. More often than not, a chief, city manager, or councilperson wants to hear anything *but* the truth.

Here it is, in all its glory. The Truth.

CHAPTER ONE

Experience is the name everyone gives to their mistakes
—Oscar Wilde

November 1979, Phoenix, Arizona. The Skulker learned valuable lessons from all seven of his arrests, and swore this would be his last one ever. He would never spend time in a cell again. Not even a few hours or so, like this time. He signed for his property, was given his court date, and was directed to the exit of the jail by the deputy. As he walked to the bus stop, he mentally reviewed his past arrests. In retrospect, he had been smart in committing the more serious crimes before he turned 18. He was 20 now, and this had been his first arrest in two years. Like his last arrest, this one had been for shoplifting. Unlike his last arrest, which was dismissed, this time he would have to go to court and would face a criminal conviction.

Getting caught was stupid. He had walked into Sears, knowing they had plain-clothed security guards watching for suspicious activity. He knew that all the mirrors were two-way surveillance locations. He had figured out approximately where the two-way mirrors were that could best observe the tool department. He had seen the undercover security guys go into the back of the tool department. He waited for them to come out and make an arrest, or go on a break, or whatever. Months before, he had seen three of them arrest a shoplifter in the parking lot, and had memorized their faces. On those trips, he had lifted some bolt cutters, channel locks, and a pry bar. When he came to pick up the tools, he waited until he saw one of the three security guys come out of the back.

He was not familiar with any of the lookout spots in sporting goods, however. He had needed some binoculars and didn't want to pay the 75-plus dollars for the good pair of Bushnell's. He had found a good hiding place to look at the house where a housewife sunbathed nude by her pool, but it was a little far away to actually see anything. With the binoculars he would be able to see everything. He would steal the binoculars, like he had the tools before. In a corner, where he checked and was sure he was not being watched, he pulled the Sears shopping bag out from under his shirt and opened it. Then he walked out the exit at the other end of the store into the parking lot, just like every other Sears's customer.

He was only 20 feet from the department store, heading towards his old Chevy pickup, when the door burst open behind him. His head automatically turned, and his stomach sunk when he recognized two of the three guys working the shoplifting detail. He did not resist or run. He knew that would make things worse. Even at that moment, he knew he would plead guilty. He tried to make this as routine and forgetful as possible for all the participants. He fully cooperated with his captors, neither being overly contrite nor totally emotionless. This was a routine arrest by the Sears shoplifting detail. He was handed over to the Phoenix Police Department, who booked, photographed, fingerprinted, and eventually released him.

His first adult arrest, the one before this one, was also for shoplifting. That had happened at an auto parts store that also sold tools. He had tried to steal a set of miniature screwdrivers, thinking that he could make lockpicks out of them. He must have looked suspicious because the owner of the store caught him putting the set into his windbreaker pocket. The cop who was called told the owner that probably nothing would happen because "the suspect never tried to leave the store." The cop wrote him a ticket but, before his court date, he received a letter in the mail stating that the county attorney had declined to prosecute due to "lack of evidence."

It was his juvenile record that would have caused him hard time, had he been over 18. At 13, he was arrested for burglarizing his seventh grade English teacher's classroom. He was caught before he was able to do what he had planned. Because Mrs. Langston had embarrassed him in front of the whole class, he was going to take a crap on her chair. When the cops caught him, he told them he had forgotten his homework assignment, which Mrs. Langston always wrote on the blackboard. This arrest was treated more as a prank than a crime. A juvenile detective "counseled" him the day his mother brought him in, and that was that. This arrest, however, did teach him about silent alarms.

Just before his 15th birthday, he had been picked up for burglarizing a home. That taught him about nosy neighbors. He thought he saw someone peek through their blinds across the street when he went into a backyard from a side gate, but ignored them. As a result of that arrest, he also learned how to con judges and probation officers through charm and guile, and how to keep a low profile during the process.

All of these lessons served him well when he was last arrested as a juvenile. He was stopped by the cops who were looking for a Peeping Tom. He had, in fact, been looking in a window of a house, where a nice-looking woman lived. He had been masturbating outside the window when he was seen by the woman's live-in boyfriend. He took off running when he heard the boyfriend come out the back door.

The boyfriend had given the cops a pretty good description of his clothing, which included a purple baseball cap. When the cops found him peeing in the bushes at a park down the street, he was taken into custody. The boyfriend could not identify him, but the cops were able to take him in anyway, as they had witnessed him urinating in public.

From this last juvenile arrest, he learned that he should do his homework to know who was living at the locations where he was peeping. He also thought it would help if he mapped out hiding places, in case he was seen. In addition, he acquired the knowledge that he should dress in a way that did not make him stand out in a crowd. He was smart enough to know these experiences would help keep him from apprehension on some of the later crimes that he just knew he could commit successfully. As he walked to the bus stop to catch the bus back to Sears to get his car, he again swore that this would be his last arrest.

He knew that his juvenile record couldn't be used against him as an adult. His first five arrests had been before he was 18. As a juvenile, the cops would take him to the Juvenile division, his mother would have to come there and get him, and then take him to juvenile court a few weeks later. The juvenile court judges considered his crimes, even the school burglaries, to be more teenage rebellion than crime, and The Skulker was never sentenced to a juvenile detention center.

CHAPTER TWO

One always has the air of someone who is lying
when one speaks to a policeman
—Charles Louis Phillippe

May 1975. The crime spree that later caused my dilemma started after I had been a police officer for six years. Ask any cop and he will tell you that you really don't start becoming an effective police officer until you have worked the field for five years. That is one reason some big city police departments get screwed up. For example, some know-it-all recruit would work out in the streets for six months until he was noticed by one of their ubiquitous ranking paper pushers, who would "rescue" the recruit from the field and make him the aide to the assistant to the adjutant to the captain of patrol. This recruit would then be one of the "golden boys," and if he (or she) could avoid stepping on his dick (or her whatever), he or she would move swiftly up the ranks.

Therein lies the present problem with most big city police departments. A large number of police administrators, with totals of six months actual time on the bricks under the protection of experienced training officers, are in charge of commanding police officers that have spent years in hand-to-hand combat with crime.

The Long Beach Police Department avoided much of the "Golden Boy Syndrome," until a new chief was selected, who came to Long Beach after doing 25 years at LAPD. But all that occurred way after I performed the retroactive abortion on the dirtbag in question, so enough about that.

After I graduated from the Police Academy, my career progressed like most other officers in the '70s. As a recruit, we were assigned a "Training Officer" for each of the first three months after graduation—one month each of working the day shift, the afternoon shift, and the graveyard shift. The Police Officers Association (POA) had recently negotiated a contract of which the major benefit was the Four/Forty work schedule—that is, patrol cops worked four ten-hour days a week.

During my first month, I worked the graveyard shift (10:30 p.m. to 8:30 a.m.) in North Long Beach with a seasoned three-year veteran training officer named Gary Fulton. Gary was an excellent, competent officer with a quiet disposition. Even though I came from a police family, I started out completely blind. I don't think I developed what cops call a "good eye" for several months.

The best example occurred a couple of weeks into my first month of training. Right after the squad meeting, while we were still driving to our beat in North Long Beach, our radio cackled and sent us (and a couple of other units) to a "415 party" in our beat. This is a loud party that is disturbing the peace of those who live nearby. At that time, if a party was generating police calls, and it was after 2200 hours (10 p.m.), we would break the party up. This particular party was being held in a house in a residential, middle class neighborhood.

The party-goers were mostly White kids with ages ranging from late teens to early twenties. They were mildly antagonistic about their revelry coming to such an abrupt end. There were beer cans and bottles littered throughout the block. As we six uniformed cops closed down the party, one of the young male merrymakers, his six-pack-induced courage overriding his sober common sense, yelled, "Fuck the Pigs." Having thus drawn attention to himself, one of the other officers at the scene immediately grabbed the loudmouth, put him in handcuffs, and walked him to a squad car. When two of his friends attempted to lynch him from the arresting officer, they were also placed into custody and cuffed. That pretty much broke up the rest of the crowd, which started meandering away from the party house.

At the tail end of this exodus, Gary pointed out a kid who was slightly staggering. We walked up behind him and told him to stop. When he turned around you could smell the odor of alcohol emitting from his breath and his clothing, which appeared to be damp from spilled beer. Swaying, he produced his driver's license which showed him to be 17 years old and that he lived a couple of miles away. We arrested him for being drunk in public. I put him in the back of our black & white and sat next to him, while Gary got in the driver's seat and headed back to the station. Gary told me as we were driving, "After we book this kid in Juvenile, we'll come back to see if the party has restarted, as they sometimes do. This is our beat, after all."

It didn't take long at the station to book the juvie and file our report, and within an hour we headed back to the party house. As we turned into the neighborhood, Gary turned off the headlights. The area looked pretty quiet. About fifty yards from the party house, I saw a young White male walking toward us. He had something in his left hand. As he brought it up, I saw what I was sure was the barrel of a gun. I yelled to Gary, "He's got a gun!" As Gary was stopping our car, this guy continued to bring up the gun I was sure he had. I was opening my door and unsnapping my holster when the fella's hand continued up to his mouth, where he took a swig from his long neck beer bottle. Rookie that I was, I thought he was going to shoot his own head off until I realized that he was holding a beer bottle instead of a gun.

We stopped him and made him pour out the rest of his beer and pick up the beer cans and bottles from in front of the house next to the party house. After he put them in a trash can at the curb, we filed a field interrogation card with his information on it and kicked him loose. When we got back in our cruiser, Gary told me that he thought it was good that I had seen something in the kid's hand and told me that he didn't fault me for saying it was a gun. He impressed upon me that it was better to be prepared for the worst, thinking it was a gun, than to be shot thinking a suspect was only pointing a beer bottle at us. He told me a good police officer will not pull the trigger until he is sure of a deadly threat.

Of all the things I learned that month from Gary (and there was a lot), what stood out the most was that "I needed to be aware and observant of the details in my surroundings."

CHAPTER THREE

Who so neglects learning in his youth,
loses the past and is dead for the future
—Euripides

June 1975. The next week, I was rotated to my second training officer, Ron Helper, who worked the afternoon shift, Watch 3, that went from 4:30 p.m. to 2:30 a.m. Ron had been on Long Beach for over seven years. His father had been a Long Beach copper, and since my dad had been a cop in neighboring Los Angeles, we instantly hit it off. I learned a lot from Ron. He was the one that taught me about there being two sides to every story. He also taught me that the police profession attracts a small but visible percentage of bullies.

Ron and I had been dispatched to a residential burglary report call. Since I was the rookie, it was up to me to write the report.

We were sitting in the parking lot of Angel's Donuts (yes, a donut shop) at Pacific and Willow when a car across the street at the gas station, an old mid-sixties brown Buick, started gunning its engine. I was writing my report and Ron was sipping on his hot chocolate (he didn't drink coffee). I would look up every so often. It was getting very annoying. Soon, I heard Ron chuckle and looked up.

It *was* kind a funny. The driver would apparently gun the engine way past the red line for a full 20 to 30 seconds, and his dog would jump out of the car, run around it, and jump back in. This went on for about 10 minutes.

"I wonder how long before this guy blows his engine up," Ron said.

"It's got to happen pretty soon," I responded.

Suddenly, the driver slammed the car into gear during a full rev and went burning rubber off the curb and into the street, turning eastbound on Willow at Mach I. The dog did happen to be in the car when the car took off like a bat out of hell. Ron immediately put our car into gear, and we followed. We didn't know if the driver was involved in a robbery of the gas station or what, but we did know that if we could see the car sitting in the gas station, the driver could also see us in a marked black & white police car… or so we thought. He must have wanted us to chase him, so we did. Ron hadn't even cleared the driveway when he turned on the red lights and siren.

Before the dimwit's Buick got to Long Beach Boulevard, it suddenly went into what looked like a panicked four wheel skid and stopped in the number one lane (that's the lane closest to the center line of the street). We found out later that the driver had inexplicably slammed the Buick into "park." Ron had just started the pursuit when this happened and so he immediately told Communications that the vehicle had stopped in the eastbound lanes just west of the Boulevard. We slowly and methodically approached the car with our guns drawn and flashlights in hand. On the passenger side of the Buick, I made a cursory look at the front passenger seat and saw that no one was sitting there. Ron was attempting to get the driver out of the driver's door he had just opened, but the dog was barking and sniping at Ron every time he tried to grab the guy. I went over to the driver's side to help Ron. Ron kept the dog away while I pulled out the now suspect of what we considered reckless driving.

This moron offered no resistance but was as limp as a noodle. This dirty-looking White boy appeared to be conscious, but just kept making bug eyes at us and would not or could not respond to anything we asked him to do. By "bug eyes," I mean his eyes were opened about as wide as they could be. I remember thinking that his eyes looked like those little kid's eyes in the paintings on black velvet that they sell in Tijuana. By the time I patted the suspect down and was handcuffing him, the first assisting unit was arriving. Franke Maranstein, who had been in my Academy Class, and his Training Officer, Todd Miles, got out of their patrol car and walked over to help us. After we put the suspect in the back of our patrol car, Todd came over and asked if we knew there was someone else in the front passenger side of the Buick. Ron and I both looked at each other, then back at Todd and Franke.

The four of us walked back to the passenger side of the Buick and there on the front floorboards was another dirty White boy. He looked as if there were no bones in his body. We all thought that he might be dead, but after we pulled him out of the car, still keeping the dog away with the nightstick, we found that he was merely suffering from the same "bug eye" affliction as his buddy, only worse. Franke and I searched, handcuffed, and carried him to my patrol car while Ron and Todd called for animal control and a tow truck.

Ron and I drove our two suspects to the Booking Tunnel. By this time, the driver was coming out of his stupefaction and Ron was able to walk him to the Booking Desk. The passenger, on the other hand, could still not stand, so I started dragging him in a modified carotid restraint hold (read choke hold) through the tunnel to the Booking Desk. Since it was a busy night and we had to park at the other end of the Booking Tunnel, I stopped with my prisoner about 12 feet outside the Booking Desk to rest. I laid the prisoner down on the concrete. At this time, a large cop I'd never seen before walked up to my prisoner and said, "It looks like he doesn't feel any pain, does he, Rookie?" Then, the big cop started walking up and down this skinny little white boy's prone body. I really didn't know what to do.

Ron saw this through the Booking Desk window and came out. Ron walked up to this cop and told him, "If you don't want to do the arrest report and book this dirtbag, Jace, you better get off him now. I don't do that shit to your prisoners." Jace smirked and walked away. Ron advised me that Big Jace had a reputation for not only bullying crooks but also other police officers. Later, Ron told me to never let another officer brutalize your prisoner. If he does, make him justify it in a report he writes.

"In other words," Ron said, "if he hits your prisoner for no reason, it's now *his* prisoner." I remembered Ron's words. On rare occasions even the most even-handed cop will lose his temper, but an extra punch or tightening of the handcuffs won't usually get a cop in trouble. It's the accumulation of such complaints that causes disciplinary action, written reprimands, suspensions, and terminations. Besides being my first experience with a brutal co-worker (and thankfully one of the few), this was my first experience with someone loaded on PCP or Angel Dust, but we didn't find that out until the dope detectives told us that later.

After filing our reports, Ron also told me that an aggressive cop will invariably receive a number of complaints. The difference is that they won't be for the same thing every time. Another one of the things Ron told me when he was training me was that it is in the street copper's best interest for brutal cops to be discovered and fired early in their careers. Ron also mentioned that the sergeants and lieutenants who were the most brutal as street cops seemed to be the most critical of any other cop using force, however legitimate.

CHAPTER FOUR

He that increaseth knowledge increaseth sorrow
—Ecclesiastes 1:18

July 1975. The next month, training took me to days (Watch 2). The day shift was completely different than afternoons or graveyard. First, the other two Watches worked two-man cars almost exclusively. On Days, the officers worked one-man cars except, of course, training units. At that particular time, the only way to get on the day shift was to either have at least seven years on the job or some compelling "hardship" reason that you could sell to the Chief of Police. As a result, most of the day Watch officers were senior patrol officers with a lot of whiskers.

With all the old timers working days, the pace of the job was a little slower. There were more traffic accidents during this shift and the day guys took their time either writing the reports, kissing them off to Watch 3 later in the day, or blowing them off completely. With all of the experience these officers had, there were enough stories to fill a library. Every day was an unending, entertaining vaudeville show of stories that were told at morning coffee, lunch (code 7), afternoon coffee, and at any call where more than one officer arrived.

This third month of training found me assigned to Dan Rouse as my training officer. Dan was a quick-witted veteran of 10 years in the Long Beach Police Department, but was considered a rookie by most of the other older officers who worked days. Dan and several other day Watch officers carried old style nightsticks with leather thongs attached and could twirl, bounce, and gyrate those sticks like no drum majorette I've ever seen. But that was just a distraction; the main event was the "war stories" these seasoned coppers told.

Almost all of the stories I heard in my early days as a cop shaped the kind of officer I became. Most were about practical jokes played on other officers or citizens or drunken sailors. The old cops who told them were some of the most interesting characters I've ever met—with Barney Elkhart topping that list.

Barney had joined the Long Beach Police Department after being discharged from the Army after World War II. Dan told me that Barney had been a paratrooper who had parachuted into France on D-Day. Dan said Barney rarely talked about his combat experience.

During my month on Day Patrol, we had code 7 with Barney at least twice a week. I heard dozens of unforgettable stories and pranks that always left Dan and me laughing. I also added several words, phrases, and acronyms to my vocabulary. I would stop Barney in the middle of a story if he referred to something that I had been unaware of until he uttered it.

Since he had been a cop for 29 years, and Long Beach had a major Naval Base, Barney had a lot of sailor stories. At one of our code 7 lunches he related a story about the Navy heyday in Long Beach. "Well," Barney started, "these downtown sailor bars were once ongoing concerns. The Pago Pago, the Circus Room, the Panama, and the Midway were busy with sailors every night of the week and packed on the weekends. You had our sailors, Australian sailors, Japanese sailors, British sailors, you name it, but mostly ours and some Marines from the ships and Navy base. When they got tired of the Pike, they would mosey on up past Ocean Boulevard and into one of the sailor bars in order to prove that a drunken human is the most stupid and pitiful of all God's creations.

"Anyway, the sailors would go to the bars because there was usually some female hangers on and some West Pac Widows that frequented those places." I stopped Barney there and asked him what a West Pac Widow was. He said, "Sorry, Rook, I forgot what ignorant slobs you rookies are. A West Pac Widow is the horny wife of a sailor assigned to the Western Pacific Fleet. After her husband's been out to sea for a month or so, or an hour or so for some, she gets an itch that needs to get scratched by some strange sailor or a cop. If you ever work the West Side, you'll get called into Navy Housing regarding a 'prowler.' Some poor sailor's wife will meet you at the door wearing a see-through negligee, with her young tits all standing up and perky, and a bullshit story about some guy peeping through her window at her. Then she'll ask you what time you get off duty and she'll want to know if you would come by after work for a beer and a little 'hide the nightstick.'"

On my last day working with Dan, he and I became the victims of Barney Elkhart's warped sense of humor. We got dispatched to the fourth floor Juvenile Bureau to talk to one of the Juvenile detectives about a kid we had arrested the day before. Barney stopped the doors from closing on the first floor and climbed aboard with us. He hit the second floor button and, just before the doors opened to let him off, he ripped an ear splitting fart and hopped off as soon as the doors opened. Before the doors could close again, two middle-aged women walked into the elevator and turned to look back toward the now closing doors. It was just as the doors came together that the odor of dead bodies, putrefied meat, overflowing sewers, and a chemical experiment gone awry entered our collective consciousness. Dan and I caught the two ladies eying each other with horrified looks and then literally exploding out of the elevator as the doors opened on the third floor. The ladies, of course, placed the blame for the noxious odor on Dan and me and the looks they passed back over their shoulders was one of such blatant hate and horror that I have seldom seen the likes of since.

CHAPTER FIVE

No notice is taken of a little evil,
but when it increases it strikes the eye
—Aristotle

February 1980. The Skulker was eating his lunch in the back room at the A1 Locksmith shop in Scottsdale, Arizona. He had been working there for a year and a month. He had befriended his boss, a lonely widower named Joe Stanley, when he had seen him at the library. He was trying to learn about picking locks. He had been in a section of the library that contained manuals for different types of mechanical devices, including a small section on padlocks, door locks, dead bolts, and the like.

He first noticed Joe's khaki uniform shirt with his first name over his shirt pocket and an A1 Locksmith patch on the shoulder. He struck up a conversation with Joe, immediately ingratiating himself to his future boss by telling him how interesting and difficult he thought it would be to become a locksmith. Joe, childless and recently widowed, was susceptible to this attention and, after speaking with him for a half hour, took him to the A1 shop and started showing him the basic elements of locksmithing. After helping around the shop without pay for a couple of weeks, Joe finally offered him a paid "internship" at minimum wage.

He didn't really care about the pay. He was still living with his mother and didn't need a lot of money. But he was ecstatic with the internship. They had been called out a couple of times for people who had locked their keys in their car trunks or in their houses. He soon realized that Joe was a master at picking all kinds of locks. In the time he had worked at A1, Joe had taught him about all kinds of locks and how to pick them, even the so-called "unpickable" locks.

Joe had also given him a set of lockpicks that Joe had made himself. They were actually more functional than commercial lockpicks. There was a complete set of picks, torsion bars, rakes, tweezers, and some key blanks that could be used on some cheap padlocks or foreign cars.

Eventually, he became aware that he had learned everything Joe could teach him. While eating lunch one day, he broke the news to Joe that he would be leaving in a week to move to Southern California. Joe did not take the information well. He had become dependent on The Skulker, both for his work and his companionship. He told The Skulker that if he stuck around, he would eventually be the owner of A1 Locksmith. He told Joe he would think about it, but he knew he had no intention of staying in the Phoenix area. In early January, he had gone to Long Beach, California and applied for a job at Southern California Edison as a meter reader.

He knew that, with his lockpicking knowledge and a job as a meter reader, he could really get into some adventures with women. He had used Joe to obtain the information and expertise he needed. Now, he was ready to begin his avocation in a more committed way. Joe was starting to get on his nerves and he was getting tired of Joe's personal quirks. When he finished his lunch, he told Joe that he wasn't feeling well and was going home early. The Skulker decided to forego his last paycheck, and knew as he walked out of the back door that day he would never return to A1.

CHAPTER SIX

They deem him their worst enemy who tells them the truth
—Plato

August 1975. After three months of training, everyone from my Police Academy Class was officially off probation. Those in charge were well aware that we still had a lot to learn, so for about the next six months we were assigned to a senior officer. My first partner was Rex Restrom.

Rex was a tall, lanky, muscular man in his mid-thirties. He was of Dutch extraction and his family had been dairy farmers in Artesia when that city was mostly rural dairy farmland. There were two key things about Rex: (1) he was a fisherman; and (2) he was pretty wealthy due to triplexes he built and rented in the Huntington Beach and Seal Beach areas. He talked about fishing and his units constantly, and if I had listened to his advice, I'd be a rich man now.

Because of his many fishing trips to Mexico each year, Rex was trying to learn Spanish. Every day, after the squad meeting, we would stop at a new little Mexican restaurant on First Street just west of Alamitos, called SuperMex. We would order a taco or two and Rex would try out his Spanish on the owner or his family.

Although Rex ate for free or half price at several other restaurants, we always paid full price at SuperMex. He would repeatedly tell me that the owners of the SuperMex (who offered us free food) were hardworking stiffs, just getting started, and we could afford to pay. When we ate at the Windrose or The Mexican Affair, though, we only paid half price because, as Rex said, they were going concerns and "didn't need our money." Rex also practiced his Spanish with the waitresses at the Mexican Affair. At those restaurants we always made up the difference and a little more in the tips we left.

It's because of working with Rex that I developed my theory that the ideal working street cop would be one who had enough money that he didn't need the job. He could go out and have all the fun of a cop without having the stress of worrying about the Brass stabbing him in the back when he did something that was perfectly legal and in policy, but looked bad to the press and/or the public. I developed this theory after I heard the story of Rex and his previous partner, Ridley Johnson.

It seems that Rex and Ridley were dispatched to a domestic dispute on Hile Street one night. Hile is a street about the width of an alley, south of Pacific Coast Highway and east of Junipero. It is lined with small, clapboard houses circa 1920. When Rex and Ridley turned onto Hile that time, they started looking for the address to which they had been dispatched. By the time they saw it they were directly across the narrow street from it. Restrom was driving and he immediately stopped the black & white. As he was getting out of the police car the dirtbag on the front porch of the house they were dispatched to started shooting at them with a handgun. Rex bailed back into the police car and followed Ridley, who had the shotgun, out the passenger door.

Using the cop car as a barrier, they started firing at the house that the suspect went into after he fired his first barrage. Almost immediately, the porch light on the house *behind* them came on. This made a bad situation worse since the back light silhouetted the two coppers for the suspect, making them an easier target. Both cops instantly realized the danger and ducked lower behind the black & white. They also both started yelling at the occupant of the porch light house to turn off the light. The only response was a crude, "Fuck you, Pigs." Not the response one would hope for in that situation.

Most people, when confronted with angry, scared police officers, do not respond in such a rude manner. Rex, thinking that the porch light endangered their lives, felt that they had to address that problem before they could effectively return fire. The suspect had resumed shooting from one of the front windows, and Rex aimed his six inch Colt .38 revolver at the porch light. After Rex missed with the first two shots, Ridley blew the porch light to Kingdom Come with one shot from the shotgun.

Right after that, they could see the dirtbag suspect reloading an old revolver while standing in the front window from which he had just removed the screen. Then, while Rex covered his back, Ridley ran across the street and fired the shotgun at the suspect, sending him into eternity when he was hit with eight of nine 00 buckshot full in the chest.

There was absolutely no problem with Ridley shooting and killing and armed suspect who was trying his damnedest to kill him and his partner, but the rude guy across the street was upset.

His porch light was disintegrated and his clapboard exterior was now decorated with two new .38 bullet holes and nine pellet holes around where his porch light used to be. He was so upset that he filed a complaint with Internal Affairs.

After completing a rather shoddy investigation, the aptly named Captain Ferret called Rex and Ridley into his office individually. Ridley went into Ferret's office first and was handed a document that turned out to be a written reprimand. It basically said that Rex and Ridley had choked under fire and had no justifiable reason for shooting out some innocent citizen's porch light. Ridley read the piece of paper, looked up at Ferret, and said, "This isn't what happened, Captain." Captain Ferret, in his most condescending and pompous voice, said, "Just sign it!"

Ridley, like most cops of that time, didn't have a pot to piss in if he lost his job, so he signed the reprimand and stalked out of Ferret's office. Rex was next and he, at least, had a hint that something wasn't right when he saw Ridley storm past him. Captain Ferret handed Rex his written reprimand that was exactly like Ridley's. Rex read it and said almost the same thing Ridley had said, "It didn't happen this way." Ferret gave the same reply that he'd given to Ridley, "Just sign it." Rex started to think that he could probably support his wife and three kids on the three triplexes he had built and was already getting rent from in Huntington Beach. His mind always was quick at calculating figures, and by the time he had signed the written reprimand, he figured he could squeak by without his police salary until he had enough money to build more apartments.

When he finished signing his name, Rex crumbled up the written reprimand, threw it in Captain Ferret's face, and stated abruptly, "That's what I think of your fucking written reprimand, Captain." Then he turned and slowly walked out of the office and to the Squad Room for the Watch 3 squad meeting, fully expecting to get called out and fired for insubordination.

In the meantime, Captain Ferret had gone directly into Chief Mooney's office demanding that he fire Rex for his verbal assault on the Captain. The Captain explained to the Chief what had transpired and Mooney, to his credit, said, "That doesn't sound like Rex. Why don't you let me handle this?" Mooney gave the Internal Affairs package to his adjutant, Sergeant Phil Brophy. When Brophy talked to all the neighbors, he found out that the jerk that had his porch light obliterated was an ex-con named Stapleton. He had been bragging to all of his neighbors that he had purposefully turned on the light so that the "psycho" across the street could "kill a cop or two before they got him."

A week and a half later, Rex and Ridley received a note from the Chief that they had done nothing wrong, that the written reprimands had been pulled from their files, and that they should be commended for a job well done.

My theory is that if Rex had not had enough rental income to challenge Captain Ferret, he and his partner would have received those reprimands and they would still be in their personnel files. But, because he had enough money to not need the police job, Rex was able to obtain justice and even had the pleasure to torque an asshole captain with impunity.

CHAPTER SEVEN

Imitation is the sincerest flattery
—Charles Caleb Colton

August 1977. It was about this time that several of my academy classmates were being involuntarily transferred to inside jobs for a year or two until the next class could replace them. The jobs consisted of the Booking Desk, Communications, Jail, and the Front Desk. The department was making the transfers by badge number, and I soon realized that I was about to be transferred to one of the inside jobs for a year or so. At that time, Rex was on vacation for about five weeks, so I was working with Danny Weaver. Danny had joined the Long Beach Police Department at the same time I did, but he had lateraled over from the Los Angeles County Sheriff's Department, where he had worked the jail for two years. It had looked like he would have to work another three years in jail before he could "hit the bricks" and work the field. He had decided to transfer to Juvenile before he was transferred to one of the less desirable inside jobs. Danny convinced me to do the same. We had a total of about two years in Patrol when we put in for the transfer. A week later, we were notified that we were on the next change of assignment. It took a total of three weeks from when we put in our transfers to the day we started Juvenile. That had to be a police department record.

Juvenile was not considered a plum assignment at that time. Juvenile detectives were looked down on by other detectives, who referred to them as "diaper dicks." Because it was hard to get officers to voluntarily transfer to Juvenile, the Department added the incentive of a modified work schedule. Everyone who didn't work patrol was on a five day/40 hour week except Juvenile. In Juvenile, detectives worked nine hour days, five days one week and four days the next. Danny and I were assigned to Watch 3 J-cars. Since we had been working Watch 3 Patrol, there was little disruption in our personal lives, except that our new days off were Sunday and Monday and every other Tuesday instead of every Tuesday.

J-cars were an innovative program that started in Long Beach. The night (Watch 3) J-cars worked out in the field from 3 p.m. to midnight, and we had to call in every couple of hours. If there was a juvenile problem somewhere in the city, we would be dispatched to handle it, if we weren't already out on another call.

Otherwise, when we called in, we would be given locations where we would have to go to contact a citizen or two about some continuing problem with kids under the age of 18. We would also go to the locations where kids hung out, drank beer, or smoked dope, and would counsel or make arrests as appropriate. It was basically a pretty good job. It entailed a lot of what I had done in patrol only we were in plain clothes (coat and tie) and in plain cars (although the hoodlums could spot a "heat short" a mile away). This actually gave us a little more freedom than working patrol. There were a couple of older detectives who worked there who were slugs and didn't want to do anything, but there were also some hard chargers in Juvenile, and that made the job a lot more fun.

We were supposed to work with one partner, but we actually got to work with everyone on the shift because when a partner worked inside you worked with another detective, and when the partner had a holiday or vacation, you worked with someone else, so we got to know and work with everybody. This was both good and bad. It was good because each detective was a little different and had his or her own way of working things. It was bad because occasionally we had to work with a slug.

There is no longer shift for a young officer or detective than to work with someone who is burned out, a drunk, or lazy… or all three. I remember working with one guy who was like that. His name was Johnny Utley. At the start of each shift, you would take whatever juveniles were in custody to county juvenile facilities. Juveniles who committed no criminal offense but were in custody because they had been abused or abandoned or their parent or parents had been arrested were taken to McClaren Hall in El Monte. Juveniles who had committed a serious crime or their parents wouldn't pick them up at our police station were taken to Los Padrinos Hall in Downey.

When I worked with Johnny, who would always start the shift driving, we would take the kids to McClaren Hall, do their entry paperwork, then take the criminal kids to Los Padrinos and do more paperwork. Then Johnny would drive us back to Long Beach, where we would go code 7 at Charlie Brown's restaurant. Johnny always ordered a "foot of martini" with his dinner. I would drive the rest of the night, which was fine with me because I could roll on hot calls I heard on the radio. This would irritate Johnny to no end. He would bitch and moan for a while, but it actually made it look to the sergeant like he was working, so he didn't gripe too much. After I had worked with Johnny two or three times a month for six months, I heard the sergeant chewing him out and telling him that he had to carry his gun with him every time he went into the field. Another detective had found out Johnny wasn't "packing heat" one night they had worked together, and Johnny had told him he never carried his gun anymore. I'd been working with a fellow police officer for six months in some of the highest crime areas in the country, and he hadn't even been carrying a gun! After working J-cars for a year, I started working the real detective end of Juvenile, both Juvenile Property Crimes and Juvenile Crimes Against Persons.

CHAPTER EIGHT

Love involves a peculiar unfathomable combination of
understanding and misunderstanding
—Diane Arbus

October 1977. While my professional life was tooling right along, my personal life was really humming. Prior to attending the Police Academy, when I was still going to Long Beach State, or as it became known while I was there, California State University at Long Beach, I was dating a nursing major named Janice Leslie. Jan was a straight-A student who lived in Westminster, only a few miles away from the college. She had a great sense of humor (one of my major requirements in a girlfriend) and, at first, we got along fine. But we had different interests and philosophies and, in truth, I wasn't mature, especially compared to Jan. After Jan and

I split up, I didn't really have a steady girlfriend, but I dated quite a bit.

After graduating from college and, later, the Police Academy, I rented a house in Seal Beach with an academy classmate and a young cop who was a veteran of two years. Like most bachelor pads of that era, we had numerous parties and I met a lot of police groupies. It was a lot of fun and gave new meaning to the term "sowing wild oats," but it wasn't particularly fulfilling. Not that I cared that much at the time.

I was the first bachelor cop in the house to fall on the matrimonial sword. After I had been out in the field about a year, but before transferring to Juvenile, I met my future wife. My regular partner, Rex, was on vacation in Mexico at the time. One night, the Sergeant teamed me up with Grant Mauw, a street cop in his forties.

His beat was East Long Beach, in an area derisively known to us hot dog young cops as "Sleepy Hollow." Our first call out of the barn after the squad meeting was a stolen car report at McDonnell-Douglas Aircraft. At the guard shack, we were directed to the Executive Offices, and from there to "Contracts." While walking some distance, Grant was telling me that there had been very few calls to McDonnell-Douglas, except for "plane movements" (when the company was moving some of their large planes from one side of Lakewood Boulevard to the other and the police were needed to stop traffic).

When we arrived at Contracts, a tall, beautiful blonde secretary was sitting behind a desk with a name plate that read Julianne Millard. She looked up and asked Grant why he was working with a Cub Scout. (I had a baby face and had been questioned before by citizens and other cops as to my legal status as a real policeman over the age of 21.) She then turned her big, baby blue eyes to me and gave me a wide wicked grin that made me tingle. I wouldn't say that it was love at first sight, but I definitely wanted to get to know this Julianne better.

She reached out, hit the intercom button, and said, "Bill, the police are here about your car." She then asked us if we wanted coffee or tea. When we declined, she gave me that smile again and a big wink, before turning back to her typing. A tall, distinguished-looking Black man with salt and pepper hair opened the door behind Julianne's desk and asked us to step in. I took the stolen car report and asked if I could use the phone. Bill got on the intercom and told Julianne to give me the "callout code," to let me use her phone, and to tell me what she had seen at lunch.

When I went into the reception area, Julianne gave me the code and the phone, and I dialed Auto Stats at the Police Department and gave them the information on the stolen Corvette. Grant stayed in Bill's office, and Julianne told me that she thought she saw Bill's car when she went to lunch with some of the other secretaries at a pizza place on Carson. It was a newer red Corvette like Bill's, but when it passed her there was a White kid with long, dirty blond hair driving it. She didn't think anything of it at the time.

At around 3 o'clock, Bill went out to get a prescription filled and came back and told her that his car was gone. I told Julianne that this was very important information, and I would need her telephone number and address for the report. She gave me both of these and said, "You're kinda cute for such a young kid." I then told her that I was nearly 25 and she told me she was a mature 27.

I called her later that night, and Julianne didn't seem the least bit surprised when I asked her out. She acted a little reluctant at first and told me she usually didn't date "young boys." After we spoke for a few more minutes, she said, "What the heck, it's not like we're gonna get married or anything." We made a date for that Sunday, since my days off at that time were Sunday, Monday, and Tuesday.

We really enjoyed each other's company and senses of humor, and seven months later we were married. Although "shacking up" was the fashionable thing to do back in the '70s, I never considered it. It was not that I was old fashioned. I had been quite a player when I was single, if I do say so myself, and of course I do. I just always thought living with a girl was kind of idiotic. If you really loved her to the point that you wanted to make her the one and only, the only logical thing to do was to marry her. And, if you didn't, why in the world would you want to give up your freedom by living together?

A few of my lifelong friends thought I couldn't have lived with the guilt, having attended Catholic schools for twelve years. My parents were both converts, so I really don't think I suffered from traditional Catholic guilt. Besides, I wanted to be married and have kids.

We were wed on the Princess Louise, which was an old ship permanently docked in the Los Angeles Harbor. (Years later it sunk. When I read about in the local newspaper, I told Julianne that all bets were off. Since the ship we were married on had sunk, our vows were no longer valid. She has steadfastly refused to acknowledge the legality of this. We are still happily married some 40 years after the ceremony and 30 years after the ship's sinking.)

It was a good thing that we did get married instead of just moving in together because we undoubtedly would not be together today. Getting to know each other is a hard thing to do, and if all you have to do is move out, it's much easier to leave. As it was, we nearly divorced each other three times that first year. Our different work schedules helped save our marriage. It is difficult to fight when you rarely see each other.

When I started working Juvenile shortly after we were wed, Sunday was our only common day off. With Julianne's work hours of 7 a.m. to 4 p.m. and mine of 4 p.m. to 1 a.m., there wasn't much time to argue, but we did make the most of it. Our disagreements went something like this:

Me: Hello, Jule.

Julianne: Hurumph.

Me: What's wrong?

Julianne: Nothing!

Me: Nothing? Then why are you acting like this?

Julianne: You should know.

Me: Well, I must be a little dense because I don't have the foggiest idea what's wrong.

Julianne: You are, of course, more than a little dense, so let me tell you even though a blind man could see the problem. We both work. You don't make the bed and I can't stand getting into a bed that hasn't been made all day. You don't put your clothes in the dirty clothes hamper. You seem to be satisfied if they land within six feet of the hamper when you toss them at it. And, on top of all that, I have to put out the trash and bring in the cans later. What exactly do you bring to this marriage?

Me (pathetically): A sizable paycheck?

Julianne (condescendingly): I make roughly a third more than you!

That being painfully true, Julianne won that argument. Our main problems were that I was a slob and Julianne was non-communicative. I had to draw her irritation out of her, and it was like pulling teeth. I was wrong in this particular case, but I will modestly reveal that I was man enough to admit it. We both worked out an equitable solution and we created a chore schedule. But Julianne didn't win all of the arguments.

On one of our mutual days off, I was reading the Sunday Long Beach Independent Press Telegram early in the afternoon. Julianne told me she had to go to JCPenney at the Lakewood Mall. She asked me to come along and said we could get a bite to eat. I had been seriously thinking of making myself a sandwich and the thought of buying a meal, rather than making it myself, appealed to me.

While we were driving to the mall, Julianne told me that, before we found a place to eat, she just needed to stop at JCPenney for a minute, to buy a pair of "nut brown colored pantyhose." We walked into the store, and Julianne immediately led me to a wall that literally held thousands of packages of pantyhose of every size and color. Julianne, who was 5'10", said she needed size large, nut brown pantyhose made by Hanes. She immediately found the correct size, brand, and color on the wall. She picked up the package, looked at it for roughly 30 seconds, then put it back in its original location.

I then watched with morbid fascination while Julianne seemed to pick up every other size, color, and brand of pantyhose on the wall. My stomach was growling, my head was aching from hunger, and here was the woman I had chosen to spend the rest of my life with, apparently doing an inventory of the complete stock of pantyhose at the JCPenney store in the Lakewood Mall. When her survey was completed, Julianne went back to the first package she had picked up, pulled it off the wall shelf, walked over to the cashier, and paid for it.

Apparently, I was standing slack jawed when Julianne looked at me, because she tilted her pretty head slightly and asked, "What's wrong with you?"

I could not hold it in. "What in the world were you doing back there? You picked out the pantyhose you said you wanted, put it back, and then looked at every other pair of pantyhose in the whole store. Then you went back and bought the first pair you looked at. Are you crazy? Are you terminally indecisive, or what?"

Sheepishly, Julianne muttered something about making sure she didn't like some other color or brand better than her "usual" brand. I think I speak for all husbands when I say that there is a complete disconnect between women and logic when it comes to shopping.

Nor does it seem to get any better with time. After Julianne and I had been married approximately seven years and had two kids, a boy and a girl, Mark and Margie, we thought it might be fun to go over to San Pedro to the Fisherman's Fiesta. This was an annual event that featured carnival rides and booths and food. We drove over the two bridges and parked our car in the parking lot for the Ports o' Call waterfront. Neither Julianne or I had been to this event before, so we didn't know exactly where to walk to get to the entrance. With a three-year-old girl and five-year-old boy in tow, we started walking across the immense parking lot toward some skylights. Julianne asked me which way we should walk, and I said it looked like we should go to the right. She said, "I don't think so, I think we should walk that way," pointing to the left. She started walking the kids to the left and, being the father and protector, I had no choice but to follow dutifully.

The Fisherman's Fiesta is a fairly large event in San Pedro, so we definitely were not the only people walking through the parking lot. Being a trained observer, I saw that roughly 60 percent of the crowd was walking to the right. The further we walked, the higher that percentage rose. This is what we in police work call "a clue." I again mentioned that I believed the entrance was to the right. She again said that she thought we were headed in the correct direction.

After another 50 yards, I once again told my beautiful but obstinate spouse that I thought we were going in the wrong direction. She again dismissed my opinion, this time with a grunt. We continued walking to the left, until there was only one other person walking in the same direction we were.

Finally, catching up to this middle-aged, well dressed gentleman, who obviously was not a fisherman, Julianne said, "Excuse me, sir, do you know where the Fisherman's Fiesta is?"

The man turned, smiled at us, and said, "Sure, over there to the right," pointing in the direction I had wanted to go all along. Julianne thanked him and we turned right and started walking in that direction. As we changed our course, I asked Julianne how long she had known the man from whom she had just obtained directions. She looked at me quizzically and said that she had never seen the man before in her life.

Now, I am not a vengeful, pushy, or condescending man, but I could not let such a victorious moment pass without comment. Triumphantly, and speaking for husbands everywhere, I burst with Biblical fervor into my lecture. "I believe I told you three separate times that we should be walking this way, but do you listen to me? Nooo. Of the billions of men in this world, you have forsaken all others to spend the rest of your life with me. Yet, when I tell you the direction I think we should go, based on my observations and experiences, both as a law enforcement officer and a graduate of a compass course provided by the U.S. Army in boot camp, you ignore me like a politician ignores a promise. But when a complete stranger, someone you yourself admit you have never seen before, gives you directions, you take it to the bank. You treat his information as though it is Gospel from the Lord on High. Why is he so credible and I'm apparently not? Now, you have to admit that you were wrong and I was right. Go on, admit it! I was right." I could hardly contain my glee. Not only had I won a large personal victory, I had struck a blow against womankind in the war of the sexes.

My joy was short-lived. Looking at me seriously, with those wonderful blue orbs that were one of my first attractions to her, Julianne said, "Stuff it, birdbrain. Even a broken clock is right twice a day." Our little boy and littler girl giggled at that. They loved it when my wife denigrated me, the Rodney Dangerfield of husbands and fathers, in front of them. But I knew that Julianne knew I had been right and had won that round, even if her counterpunch had scored.

CHAPTER NINE

The penalty for laughing in a courtroom is six months in jail.
If it were not the penalty, the jury would never hear the evidence
—H.L. Mencken

September 1979. The murderous, cutthroat rapist whose demise I facilitated started his attacks after I returned to patrol from Juvenile. I had been trying to get back to Patrol for a year. I had worked three years in Juvenile: one year in night J-cars, six months in day J-cars, and another year and a half in Juvenile Investigations. Investigations gives a cop a working knowledge of what the assistant district attorneys need to file on suspects to get convictions. I felt I had the perfect experience to go back to Patrol and become an excellent field cop. Also, I would be working one day less every other week, since Patrol worked a four/forty schedule as opposed to Juvenile.

The first opening available to me was on Watch 1, the graveyard shift, from 10:30 p.m. to 8:30 a.m. I had a good partner with whom I enjoyed working, and it was a good, busy beat, but I hated working those hours.

The two things I remember most working the graveyard shift were 1) I was almost always red-eyed, tired, and surly, and 2) the inside of my eyelids always felt like sandpaper. Some really like working that shift, but they are better men and women than I am. A lot of those guys would work their four days and then stay awake all day on their first day off, to get back into a "sleeping at night" mode. I could never do that. If I slept four hours on a particular day, it was a great day. I would come home from work at roughly 9 a.m., dog tired, and go right to bed. I would drop off to sleep and wake up at 10:30 a.m., go back to sleep and suddenly wake up and it would be 11:45 a.m. This would go on until 2 or 2:30 p.m., when I could not get back to sleep and I would finally get out of bed. That was on the days that I didn't have court.

By this time in my career, I had testified in court in around a hundred or so cases. I had learned of the traps set by defense attorneys the hard way, and by this time had become pretty adept at anticipating and deflecting them to the benefit of the prosecution. Defense attorneys try to do to cops what a good interrogator does to a suspect. In other words, lock the cop into a story and pull the rug out from under him.

For instance, you see a suspect running away from a liquor store with a brown paper bag in one hand and a gun in the other. You and your partner chase that suspect who you believe is wearing a white jacket and black pants. You put out a description of him on the police radio as male, White, early twenties, six feet, wearing a white jacket and black pants. The suspect tosses the gun over a fence and it lands in a puddle of water, thus effectively ruining any prints. You don't have time to stop for the gun, but you mark the location in your mind. You lose sight of him as he rounds a corner. As you cautiously round the corner, you see him stand up from a kneeling position near some bushes and start to run again, but by this time you are close enough to tackle him, overcome whatever resistance he presents, and handcuff him. You get back on the radio and code four (no further assistance necessary) the incident.

As you walk the suspect back to your black & white, you stop at where he was kneeling in the bushes, and you find a brown paper bag with cash of several denominations in it. You also stop where he tossed the gun over the fence and either you or your partner, or an assisting unit, jumps over the fence and retrieves the gun.

When you book the suspect in at the Booking Desk, you inventory his clothing. In the florescent light, you realize that he is wearing a bright yellow jacket and green pants. The discrepancy between the colors is due to the fact that the streetlights in Long Beach are mercury vapor lamps that put out a distinctive yellow tint that makes the accurate identification of colors at night impossible. A very experienced and conscientious officer will note the street lighting in his report, but most officers would not even think about it. In an honest recitation of the facts, street lighting does not always seem important, but in the courtroom it is very important.

After you testify on direct examination, answering the prosecutor's questions, the defendant's lawyer will cross-examine you. He is trying to plant seeds of doubt with the jury. He will ask you several questions about your report. He will ask you what you saw in the hope that it will vary, however minutely, with your report. He will ask what the suspect you saw running from the liquor store was wearing, hoping that you will describe the suspect's clothing at the time of booking, rather than the description you put out on the police radio.

If you do, the defense attorney will be sure to point out the difference in the clothes the defendant was wearing at the time of his arrest and the description you put out on the radio. He will also point out that when his client was arrested he had neither a gun nor the money from the liquor store. He will indicate to the jury that you lost sight of the suspect you *originally* saw when he turned the corner, thus leaving the impression with the jury that you were mistaken when you arrested his client, who was wearing different colored clothing than the liquor store robber you originally saw. And when he makes his summation to the jury, his client's defense will be that it was a case of mistaken identity or, worse, that you couldn't find the real robber so you settled for the nearest innocent bystander.

It has been my experience that the defense attorneys who are polite and infer mistakes on the part of law enforcement, rather than intentional misconduct, win much more often than the firebrands who claim police conspiracy. Even the most anti-police ignorant juries find it easier to believe a cop made an honest mistake than he and/or the victim and/or the prosecutor and/or anyone else conspired to arrest and prosecute someone they had never seen before. Of course, if the officer had arrested the suspect before, or if the suspect had filed a complaint against the officer prior to or even after his arrest, the suspect's lawyer will try to bring that up in court so he can show the jury that the cop had it in for his client.

My partner on graveyard was John Transom. He was a couple years older than I was but had a year less on the job. John had the advantage, however, of having spent all of his time in Patrol, so he acted as my training officer to get me back up to snuff on patrol procedures. He was 5'10" and weighed roughly 180 pounds. He was balding and a little intense, and had earned the nickname "Cadet," short for "Space Cadet," due to his looks and an affinity for science fiction books and movies. He talked me into going to see the movie "Alien," and we talked about how it scared the hell out of both of us. He was also an ardent baseball fan, and we spent hours together talking about the Angels and the Dodgers.

Working with John provided me with the incident where I had the most fun testifying. Early one Sunday morning, just before sunrise, a call went out for unit One Adam Three (1A3) (a downtown unit) to handle a suspect who was attempting to pass a counterfeit $10 bill at the Norm's Restaurant at Pacific Coast Highway and Long Beach Boulevard. 1A3 was manned by Larry Lawrence and his rookie partner. Larry was a great officer but sometimes he did not want to be bothered with petty crimes. Apparently, this call wasn't important enough for Larry to handle. He got on the radio and said, "Don't you show me code Five (staked out) on a twenty thousand and one (felony hit and run) suspect vehicle?"

The dispatcher told Larry and his partner that she thought the call they were on was a twenty thousand and two (a misdemeanor hit and run with no injuries). He told her that there *were* injuries and he and his partner were "sitting on" the suspect vehicle at Magnolia and 21st Street. We later found out that the injuries consisted of the victims "complaining of pain." The operator then called our unit, to respond to Norm's. This was way out of our beat, but it was really slow in our area, so we gave our location and started heading halfway across the city to Norm's. The dispatcher advised us that the suspect was a male Black, with a black afro, brown eyes, and was 5'8", 140 pounds, wearing a dirty white t-shirt, dirty khakis, and black tennis shoes.

When we arrived at Norms, we pulled into the back parking lot and walked up to the entrance, trying to avoid the windows so as not to telegraph our arrival. When we walked in the front door, the hostess motioned with her head toward our right. When we looked, it was obvious who our suspect was. There was a booth with a long table in the rear of the restaurant. There were eight Black males sitting at the table. They were all dressed in suits and ties. To me, it was obvious they were having a quick breakfast before church services. They were all looking incredulously at the suspect, dressed in his dirty white t-shirt and dirty khakis.

We walked back to the table and I asked one of the suits if they knew the fellow sitting at the end of the table in the white t-shirt. One of them said that the guy just came over and sat down and that they, the men in the suits, had nothing to do with him or whatever he had done.

John pulled the suspect out of the booth and started patting him down for weapons and any counterfeit money. While John was doing that, one of the other men at the table told me that the suspect had shoved something between the cushions in the booth. I gingerly reached between the cushions and felt what seemed to be a piece of paper. I pulled out a poor imitation of a $10 bill. John handcuffed the suspect and told the dispatcher that we had the suspect in custody.

Before the dispatcher could acknowledge John, the radio cackled with the voice of Larry Lawrence, who said, "One Adam Three, we'll be en route to pick up our prisoner."

John responded instantly. "Negative, One Adam Three. We're already ten-fifteen (en route to jail with a prisoner)."

Larry then said, "It's our beat, we'll handle it."

John got right back at Larry with "You've got nothing to handle now—unless you would like to take the nine sixty-one (report)." Larry liked to make a lot of arrests and get a lot of court time, but he (like a lot of other officers) wasn't much interested in "taking paper," i.e., writing reports.

Larry could not let John have the last word, so he countered, "Negative on that, you've got the whole thing, you poachers."

We weren't really "en route to the station." I was up for the report so I had to talk to the hostess, to whom the suspect had tried to pass the phony bill, and all of the men at the booth where the suspect had so inadequately tried to camouflage himself. I quickly obtained the pertinent information and we were really en route.

While John drove us back to the station, I read the suspect his rights. To the first waiver question, "Do you understand these rights I've explained to you?" the suspect answered "Yes." To the second waiver question, "Having these rights in mind do you wish to talk to me now?" The suspect answered "No." We arrived at the station, booked the prisoner, and filed our arrest report and the evidence.

Because of the small amount of the counterfeit bill, and no evidence of any other similar type of funny money finding its way to our area of Southern California, the Secret Service declined to file criminal charges against our suspect. (We, of course, told Larry that this suspect had been spreading these bills all over the Western United States, and the Secret Service wanted us to testify in Seattle. Larry just shook his head and said, "You damned poachers.")

The suspect was, however, on parole for armed robbery so we were subpoenaed to go to the Los Angeles County Jail for a parole board hearing. The hearing was held in a makeshift courtroom on the first floor of the county jail. The suspect's Parole Agent acted as the prosecutor.

There were three Parole Board Members who acted as judges and jury, and a Los Angeles County Sheriff Deputy acted as a bailiff. The defendant and his attorney sat at a table to the left of the prosecuting Parole Agent.

The "proceedings" started with the Parole Agent telling us that this was basically an informal setting but would be conducted much like a trial. Witnesses were advised to wait outside. While John was outside, I testified as to what happened and to the facts in my report. When the Parole Agent was done asking questions, the middle of the three Parole Board Members told the suspect's attorney he could cross-examine me.

After a few perfunctory questions, this attorney asked me if I had read his client his rights. I told him that I had. Then he asked me what the suspect's responses were. I told him that the suspect stated that he knew and understood his rights and that he did not want to speak to me at that time.

The attorney then asked me, "And why do you think he didn't want to speak to you?"

I was immediately taken aback by this question. I could not believe that an attorney would ask such a question. I didn't know where he was going or what he was up to. I was so incredulous that I asked him, "Are you asking for my opinion?"

The parolee's attorney said, "Yes, why do you think my client didn't want to talk to you about his arrest?"

I couldn't suppress my smile. Gladly, I answered, "I guess he wanted to talk to some shyster lawyer like you before he said anything to a cop."

The Parole Agent started laughing, the Parole Board Members started laughing, the parolee started laughing, and the Sheriff Deputy/Bailiff started laughing and pumped his right arm, mouthing the words "all right." The parolee's attorney jumped up, slammed his hand down on the table, and yelled, "He's impugning my dignity as an officer of the court. He is defaming my reputation. He's…." You get the picture. The attorney's raving went on for at least half a minute or so, until the head of the Parole Board finally told him, "You asked for his opinion, counselor." I was asked a few more questions and then dismissed. I think that attorney would have tried to punch me if given half the chance.

John testified after I left the room, but he was only in there ten minutes. As we walked back to our car, John asked me what I had said in there. He said everyone was still chuckling when he walked in. When I told him, John laughed himself silly and told me he wished he had said that.

CHAPTER TEN

Tolerance is the virtue of the man without convictions
—G.K. Chesterton

November 1979. Generally speaking, I'm an easy-going guy. There are some cops who won't work with certain other cops because they think they are unsafe, or they piss people off for no reason. I have been able to work with almost everybody. If an officer I was working with was unsafe, I would explain to him or her why what he or she did was unsafe, and how to correct it. Most people want to do a good job and if you present a deficiency to them in the right way, they will take it constructively and make the correction, especially when so advised by a senior officer.

There has only been one officer in my career that caused me to go to the sergeant and tell him to "never, ever put me with that asshole again." John was on vacation and for a week or so I had been working with a different partner every night. On one particular night, the squad sergeant assigned me to work my regular unit 2A9 with a fellow named Guy March. I had seen him two or three days a week in our squad meetings, but I had never worked with him before. He had a reputation as a know-it-all hard charger. I had only a vague impression that he was kind of an arrogant prick, but I was willing to give him the benefit of the doubt. I shouldn't have. He had only been in the department two and a half years at that time and was much too junior to be so swaggering.

After the meeting, I got behind the wheel of our squad car and planned to drive the first part of the shift. As I was driving through Area One to our beat in Area Two, a dispatcher came on the radio, "Any unit, 415 (disturbing the peace), shots, area of Bonito and Broadway." Even though we were already past that section of the city, Guy grabbed the microphone and said, "Two Adam Nine, we'll handle that from 4th and Walnut."

I turned our black & white south on Walnut to Broadway and then pulled up across the street from the El Toro Bar. There were two older White males standing on Bonito two houses north of Broadway. After a moment of listening and not hearing anything, Guy and I got out of our car and approached the two older gentlemen. As we were walking up to them, Guy told me that he usually worked this area and that "the Mexicans are always shooting up the Mexican Bar." The two old guys did not look like they posed an immediate threat, but I kept my eyes on their hands just in case.

We asked them what had happened. They told us that a green '69 Chevy Malibu, containing two Mexican males, had pulled up across the street from the El Toro and had fired a chrome revolver out of the right passenger window into the air, and then had driven westbound on Broadway then north on Alamitos. They also told us that this had happened about 10 minutes before we showed up. We thanked them for the information and went back to our police car. As I started to drive away, I reached for the mic with the intention to put out the suspect vehicle description and direction of travel, so the Area One units might know that car quite possibly contained a gun and had fired shots in the air. Before I could grab the mic, however, Guy grabbed it and broadcast, "This was just a bunch of Mexicans shooting up the Mexican bar here again, ten-eight" (we are back in service).

I glared at him and asked, "Why'd you say that? That isn't what happened."

"They're always shooting up that Mexican bar," Guy responded.

I couldn't believe it. "Well, that isn't what happened this time, Buddy."

Before Guy could respond, the Area One sergeant put out on the radio that the unit that had just checked ten-eight from the shooting call should go back and take a report for shooting into a building. I continued to glare at Guy while he again picked up the mic and asked if we could "10-87" (meet) the sergeant at 4th and Orange (Winchell's Donuts). When we met the sergeant, Guy started tap dancing and told the sergeant exactly what had happened and how "the Mexicans were always shooting up that bar."

"That isn't what happened this time, though," the sergeant said.

"That's what I told him," I added helpfully.

"Well, don't do that again. If the suspects aren't shooting into an inhabited building, don't put it out that way." I could not have agreed more. (STRIKE ONE!)

After Guy put out the vehicle and suspect description, and that shots had been fired into the air and not the bar, we again headed out to our beat. Next, we handled a residential burglary report that Guy took. After Guy got the information, I started heading toward Community Hospital. They had a room where officers could sit at a desk and write out a report, or phone it in to one of our "electronic stenos" that would tape record a verbal report, and a human steno would transcribe it later. While driving there, Guy, who I grudgingly admit had a pretty good eye, said, "Doesn't that red Ford Fairlane look like a deuce?" (The California Vehicle code section for a drunk driver was originally 502 and ever since then 'a deuce' has indicated a drunk driver, in California police parlance.)

I started following the Ford and observed it as it straddled the lanes and weaved ever so slightly. The car was also traveling a good 10 miles an hour below the speed limit, which in Long Beach was enough probable cause to stop it. I turned on my flashing lights and the Ford continued for three blocks before the driver seemed to notice us behind him. He was in the number one lane (the one closest to the center line). He pulled into the number two lane, and stuck his arm out of the window, motioning for us to pass him. I pulled in behind him and gave the siren a quick burst before the driver finally pulled the Ford to the curb and stopped. As I was getting out of our car, the driver started to get out of the Ford. He stumbled a little and started to walk toward me, swaying just a little. When he was about three feet away he asked, "What's the problem, officer?" I could already smell the odor of alcohol.

I gave him the standard police Field Balance and Coordination test. He was under the influence, but not too badly. I arrested and handcuffed him and put him in the back of our patrol car. We didn't have cages in the back of our cars then, so the passenger officer had to ride in the backseat with the prisoner, to control him if the prisoner got out of line. Guy got in the back with him. Our prisoner was an amiable enough drunk, but Guy started chipping at him. I could tell that the prisoner was starting to get pissed, so I told Guy to knock it off and he reluctantly shut up.

At the Booking Desk, Guy administered the Breathalyzer test. I thought the prisoner would blow a .12 or .13 blood alcohol. The legal limit in California at that time was .10. Guy guessed the guy would blow a .15 or .16. We were both surprised when he blew a .29. I knew that I couldn't even stand if I was over a .20 blood alcohol, but this guy was actually maintaining fairly well. He certainly didn't look that drunk. The Booking Desk Sergeant told us that longtime alcoholics can maintain better than ordinary people. That is, until they reach a certain point in their drinking careers, and then one little beer gets them blitzed.

We booked our drunk driver, filed our arrest report, and started back out in the field. This time, it was Guy's turn to drive. For half an hour after we left the station, Guy drove his regular beat in Area One. I finally told him to get back to our assigned beat, east of Cherry, and he mumbled something about checking out one more location. From 7th Street, Guy turned north onto Orange Avenue. A block south of 10th Street, we could see the traffic light for us turn from red to green. Right after that we saw a beat up white 1964 Plymouth Valiant turn south onto Orange from west on 10th running the red light for east/west traffic on 10th Street.

Guy asked the rhetorical question, "Did you see him run that red light?" and then stopped right in the middle of the block. I thought he was going to let the Valiant pass us and then make a U-turn and pull him over for a ticket. I was wrong. As the Valiant approached us, we could see that it contained two long-haired dirty White boys of the motorbike type (Hell's Angels, Hessians, etc.). I couldn't believe my eyes when, as the car passed, Guy put our patrol car in reverse and, at thirty miles an hour and accelerating, yelled for them to pull over.

By the looks of them, I was sure they had just pulled an armed robbery and were going to start blasting us with the sawed-off shotgun I was sure they had on the seat next to them. And the lunatic who was driving our car was giving these dirtbags ample opportunity by keeping pace with them while driving backwards! I had my hand on the door handle and was ready to bail at the first sight of a weapon. Surprisingly, the dirtbags in the Valiant stopped. Of course, Guy stopped right next to them. I couldn't get out of the car fast enough. Guy opened his door and squeezed between our car and the Valiant, and then ordered both the driver and passenger out of the car and to the front of our patrol car. While they stood at the front of our car, Guy first shined his flashlight into the Valiant and then patted both of the dirtbags down for weapons. I stood and watched all of this from behind my open door. Fortunately, these two guys were very cooperative and did everything Guy told them to do. He wrote the driver a ticket, ran both of them for warrants, then kicked them loose.

When Guy got back into our car, he saw me glaring at him for the second time that night. He asked, "What's wrong?"

"That was the most unsafe traffic stop I've ever seen." Then I let him have it with both barrels. "Not only could you have gotten us killed by backing into someone who was pulling out of their driveway, but didn't you think those two dirtbags looked a little hinky? They looked to me like they had just robbed a liquor store or something. And you're backing up right next to them, window to window? If you ever do anything like that again, if the bad guys don't shoot you, I will!" Guy reluctantly admitted that he had made safer traffic stops, but did think he was excellent at backing up a car. (STRIKE TWO!)

In Long Beach, calls for service would start to die down around a quarter to three in the morning. The bars closed at 0200 hours (2 a.m.), and by 0300 (3 a.m.) most of the drunk drivers were either going to jail, had successfully snuck under police radar and were at home sleeping, or were at Hof's Hut drinking coffee and ordering breakfast. By 0330 (3:30 a.m.), all of the family disputes between the drinkers and their spouses were resolved one way or another, and most of the city was effectively put to bed.

At about 0430 hours (4:30 am), we were in the Granada Beach Parking lot, by the Belmont Pool, and I was driving east just past the pool. A 17 or 18 year old Mexican kid and his girlfriend were sitting on the two-foot-high concrete block wall that separated the parking lot from the sand. I stopped the squad car a good 20 feet from them. When they saw us, it looked like the kid set something down in the sand, grabbed his girlfriend's arm, and started walking away from us. Guy jumped out of the car and yelled for the kids to stop, which they did. Guy and I walked up to them and, before I could ask for their IDs, Guy asked the kid what he had left on the beach. The kid apprehensively told us, "Nothing, sir."

Guy turned around and walked back to where the two kids had been sitting. When he returned, he had a small brown paper bag that had a half empty can of Budweiser in it. Guy walked up to the kid and, right in front of God and everyone, hit the kid in the face with the back of his hand. He then grabbed the kid by the front of his shirt and said, "You don't ever lie to the police." At this point, I had had enough of this badge-heavy little prick. I just shook my head, walked back to the black & white, and sat down in the driver's seat.

Guy yelled at the kid for another minute or two, made him pour out the rest of the beer, and sent him and his girlfriend on their way. When he got back in the squad car he said, "I hate liars. That's why I pimp slapped him. You're not pissed about that, are you?"

"Yeah, I'm pissed off! Don't we have enough people who hate us without giving that kid and his girlfriend an actual reason to? And here's a big surprise, shithead. 95 percent of the people we talk to lie to us. If you slapped everybody who lied to us, your hand would fall off and they would dedicate a whole floor to you in Internal Affairs. And while we're on that subject, I want you to know something. I don't lie. I don't lie in court and I don't lie in Internal Affairs. So, on the off chance that kid files a complaint against you and they ask me what I saw, I'm gonna tell 'em." I wasn't done, however. I continued, "What the fuck is the matter with you? You never drank beer when you were underage? You never lied to a cop or your parents or a teacher? You're a saint? I oughta slap you silly, you short little obnoxious prick! What a big brave thing to do. You slapped a kid two inches shorter and 30 pounds lighter than you. Would you have slapped a 6'4" USC middle linebacker? I doubt it." (STRIKE THREE, YOU'RE OUT!)

"None of my other partners have had a problem with the way I do my job," Guy whined.

"Just shut up," I snarled.

The rest of the night was quiet. Before the squad meeting the next day, I asked the sergeant to never partner me with Guy again. Guy continued working, got into some trouble with Internal Affairs, and received a few two- and three-day suspensions. I occasionally heard that he was still heavy-handed, but he was intelligent enough not to get caught on the big stuff. Thankfully, he never made rank.

If I had gone to Internal Affairs, Guy might have received a few days suspension—if he told the truth, which I think he would have after we had our little talk. However, he also would have bad-mouthed me and called me a snitch, which would have necessitated me kicking his obnoxious little ass. On the Long Beach Police Department, at least at that time, if you fought another police officer or challenged him to fight, while on duty or in uniform, you were subject to losing your job.

Second, the vast majority of officers would have thought that Guy's backhanding was chickenshit, but it wouldn't have given them much dyspepsia. The police culture of the time rationalized that "street justice" had to be dispensed by cops because the courts and penal systems certainly weren't punishing anyone. So a few "floggings" were administered.

Also, the courts at that time were well into the early stages of judicial activism. The Miranda decision was a little over a decade old. The court-imposed "rules of evidence" were changing daily, as were the different courts' "interpretations" of what constituted probable cause. It seemed to us street cops and detectives that, no matter how logically we explained stopping a car or a person, if it later led to an arrest, the courts would rule that we had insufficient probable cause for the stop.

The appellate courts were throwing out convictions left and right. There was even a case where a police officer saw a guy carrying a big TV down the street and, when he saw the cop, dropped the TV and started running away. The cop chased this suspect down and held him while another unit checked around and found a house in the area that had been burglarized. An appellate court later threw the conviction out because two out of three appellate court justices felt that there was no probable cause to stop the suspect "just because he dropped the television and ran away when he saw the cop." Only a moron, an ACLU attorney, or an appellate court judge wouldn't have considered that probable cause.

Maybe my problem is that I try to think too logically. I always thought that the objective of a criminal justice system is to do justice in criminal cases. I thought that meant guilty people would be found guilty and would be punished, and innocent people would be set free. How wrong I was! Things are at least marginally better now, but at that time, the objective of the system was to make sure that the government and its agents played by the rules, even though the rules changed hourly, and differed depending on whether it was a state or federal appellate court that was making and/or changing the rules.

From one week to another, cops never knew if they could search a vehicle for items taken in a robbery after arresting the robbery suspect who was stopped in that vehicle, or if they had to get a search warrant for that vehicle. They never knew for sure if they were just talking to someone on the street if it was a "detention," which required them to read the person his rights, or if it was a conversation of which contents could be used later in court, if that person were to be arrested for a crime. Laws were constantly changing and evolving, and cops were the last ones to know. This made our job incredibly difficult.

CHAPTER ELEVEN

No one ever suddenly became depraved
—Juvenal

February 1980. The Skulker considered himself the Midnight Skulker. He'd read the name in one of the comic strips in the newspaper. But he wasn't funny, and people wouldn't be laughing when they found out what he was doing. Especially the women. He didn't like women. Women were pushy and demanding, and the more they pushed and demanded, the more pissed off he got. But when they were frightened, women were more tolerable. In fact, when they were really afraid, they excited him. Like the two women in Phoenix. He got hard just thinking about them. The second one had really been shaken and that made it all the better. But he had to admit that he had already been aroused before his thoughts turned to Phoenix.

Walking around in the shadows, looking in the lighted windows, watching women who had no idea they were being watched, that was what really turned him on. He knew he was good at it—skulking, that is. And he was smart. He researched. He studied what he considered "the arts": the art of camouflage at night, the art of moving without making noise, the art of lockpicking, the art of entering silently through windows and doors, and the art of burglary.

He'd read military books and manuals on reconnaissance. He'd read accounts of cat burglars. He'd studied books on surveillance. He'd made ample use of the Long Beach City Library looking up books, periodicals, and newspaper articles about anything to do with stealth, disguise, illegal entries, the collection of evidence, and crime scenes. He planned and reconnoitered and classified his possible victims, their homes, and their neighborhoods. He learned from his mistakes.

He knew from reading the biographies and autobiographies of military men that a nighttime mission was always preceded by a daylight reconnoitering to familiarize the troops with the geography and topography of the area. His prior job in Phoenix, where he had trained and worked as a locksmith, had helped prepare him for what he thought of as his avocation. His current job in Long Beach, as a meter reader for Edison, was perfect. It helped him in two ways: learning all of the alleyways, hiding places, and best escape routes, and being paid while getting all his "intelligence."

He could hardly wait for what he thought of as his next adventure. But he was patient. He knew he had to lay the proper groundwork before he had his fun. During the past week, he had gone about his job. While he conscientiously read and recorded each house's meter, he was also taking notes that would help him later determine where the best victims lived, which houses were the most vulnerable, which homes had dogs, which dogs were friendly and which weren't, and the best escape routes and alternatives.

If he found that a potential victim was married or had a live-in boyfriend, he rated her down to a secondary status, reasoning that a husband/boyfriend might be an undue complication that would have to be overcome to avoid apprehension. He didn't eliminate her from the list of possible victims, he just moved her down on the list, feeling his time would be better spent finding out about women who lived alone. He might move her up again if he found out that her "man" worked nights or traveled a lot.

He learned another valuable lesson from his day job. In his Edison uniform, he was virtually invisible. He walked through neighborhoods where people would call the cops on anyone even remotely suspicious, yet no one took notice of him. He knew he was pretty nondescript anyway. At 5'9" tall and weighing 160 pounds, he was of average height and weight. His brown hair and brown eyes added to his commonness. Put on the Edison shirt and he was going through people's front and back yards just like H. G. Wells' *Invisible Man*. Even when people looked right at him, they didn't see him. They saw the Edison man. It really was the perfect job.

This night he was doing reconnaissance, having already completed his survey while working earlier that day. He worked this East Long Beach neighborhood the middle of each month for Edison. It was a middle-class neighborhood, consisting of tract houses that had been built after World War II to accommodate returning veterans and new aircraft manufacturing employees at Douglas Aircraft. These houses had been here a little over 30 years, so the banal sameness of tract houses had long ago faded with room additions, different veneers, growing shrubs, and individual landscaping.

He knew the five basic floor plans of the original houses and could make pretty good educated guesses on what the additions would do to those floor plans. People with the same floor plans tended to have similar additions. All of the original homes had large backyards and fair size front yards, so most people added to the back of their houses, usually more bedrooms for growing families, but also large family rooms. A few homeowners had decided to add upwards, but there were very few two-story houses in this section of Long Beach.

He was seeing which of his possible victims was home at 12:30 a.m., which ones were Watching television or had lights on, what the possible hiding places looked like at night, and which areas might provide "cover and/or concealment" at night that were not readily apparent during daylight hours. He also wanted to know where the shadows fell as the result of the streetlights, porch lights, and ambient lights from windows. He had to make mental notes because he didn't have his notebook, and he couldn't write in the dark anyway. He would put them in his notebook later.

He saw a light on in what looked like a back bedroom, right at the backyard fence of a gray house, two houses in from the corner. He walked in a natural manner, looking to see if there was anyone else on the street or if anyone was glancing out their windows. He didn't see anyone, so he walked over to a huge drooping pepper tree that was on the south side of the gray house not too far from the lighted window. From this vantage point he was completely hidden in an enveloping shadow. He could easily see the window, but all he could see of the room was part of one blank wall. He could detect motion in the room like someone was moving around, but then again it could just be a reflection from a television. If he wanted to see who was in the room, he would have to move closer to the fence and away from his concealment.

He suddenly remembered who lived in that house and his hard-on grew. The woman was a reasonably attractive, small-breasted redhead, slightly overweight, with attractive freckled skin. But that wasn't what increased his ardor. What got him going was the fact that she was a pushy, overbearing, obnoxious bitch. When he had been making his Edison rounds the month before, he had seen this woman loudly castigate her next-door neighbor for allowing his cats to roam the area. He was an elderly gentleman who seemed to shrink with her every word. "Now, Nan, what do you want me to do? They're cats. You can't train cats. They won't sit or stay or roll over like dogs."

"I don't really care what you do, Sam, but if I catch any of your cats digging up my flowerbeds again, I'll roll my car over them, or you if you get in my way." The emasculating whore needed to be brought down a peg.

He moved slowly and deliberately out from under the tree and closer to the fence to get a better angle into her room, keeping his eyes on the window. He realized that he was a little more exposed here, not from the street, but from her lighted window and the front porch windows of the old man's house next door. He wasn't worried about the old man or his house though. Those lights had been off since he had arrived.

As he edged closer to the fence, his view of the room inside the window expanded. Halfway to the fence, he saw the woman in profile as she slipped a flannel nightgown over her nude body. He just caught a glimpse of one of her pink nipples as the gown slid down. Dammit, if he had been a few seconds faster, he would have really seen a show.

This excited him even more and, in this state, he lost some of his caution and started moving a little faster toward the shadow of the fence. He had almost reached it when he tripped on a sprinkler head and fell with a loud crash into the wooden fence. As he was picking himself up, the woman appeared in the window and looked him right in the face. He was about 12 feet away, but it felt like she was right up close to him. As he started running away, he heard a scream that was partly muffled by the closed window.

He knew that she would call the cops and that they would come swarming. He was afraid but told himself he was being irrational. Even though he felt that "Nan" looked right at him, he doubted that she would be able to identify him because she was in a lighted room looking out a glass window into the darkness. Even so, if stopped by the cops, he didn't want to have to explain why he was three or four miles from his own home at a quarter to one in the morning. He knew that cops in Long Beach would hustle him to jail if they couldn't find anyone else to blame for the "peeping," and he didn't want to have to leave Long Beach altogether.

He knew from the books he had read on police procedures that the cops would come and set up a perimeter and stop anything and everything that was moving. He also knew from reading the Independent Press-Telegram that Long Beach was an under-policed city, having fewer cops per thousand than other cities. He figured he had six or seven minutes before cop cars started arriving. He knew where he had to go and what he had to do.

He ran away from where he had parked his car. He continued running two blocks north and then turned east at a corner and slowed to what he was sure looked like a leisurely walk. He turned into an alley, walked south half a block, then quietly opened a redwood stake fence gate that he knew was unlocked. He had this address pre-scouted as one of the best hiding places in this neighborhood if he needed one. It was a house that was vacant while it was under construction. The backyard had been dug up and a new foundation poured. Since he had last seen the backyard two days ago, the carpenters had already laid the subfloor for what looked like a new master bedroom, bath, and family room. He was glad the subfloor was down because that made it easier to get to the old back door without tripping over the foundation footings.

He tried the sliding glass door next to the old wooden back door, but after jostling it silently for a moment, he figured the workers had put a broomstick handle in the track to secure it. He couldn't see it in the darkness but that's what it felt like. He was sure that he could eventually work the door open, but he had his lockpicks with him so he saw no need to chance making any noise with the slider that might arouse any of the neighbors. He also knew that the lock on the wooden door was an older common tumbler lock that he could easily pick. He had practiced picking such locks in the dark and knew he could do it now.

He pulled out his picks that were secreted in the bottom seam of his jacket. He put the tension bar in place and thought that if he used a rake he could probably line the pins in the tumbler of such an old lock with a couple of passes, but he pulled out a regular pick because he felt he was in no hurry and could use the practice in the darkness. Even with that he opened the door in less than 30 seconds. He quickly and quietly entered the house, closed the door, and stood leaning against the wall, letting his eyes adjust to the even darker room inside. He re-locked the door and waited.

He had a penlight, but didn't want to use it because some of the windows weren't covered, and even the slightest moving light, if seen by a neighbor, would alert the cops to his location. While he closed his eyes and waited, he put his picks back into their leather pouch and into the hidden seam pocket. He opened his eyes after roughly a minute and realized that it wasn't nearly as dark as he'd expected. Streetlights from the front of the house shined through the uncovered living room window and that light brought some illumination into the kitchen where he found himself. Looking into the living room, he was able to see that the owners had left their furniture covered with sheets.

He saw a hallway on the other side of the living room and moved stealthily toward it. He looked down the hall and saw three open doors. Some light could be seen coming from the closest room to the front of the house, and from the linoleum floor he surmised it was the bathroom. He edged his way past the bathroom, staying away from any light just for practice, then went into the next room which was a bedroom. There was a bed in the middle of the room, also covered with a plastic drop cloth. He walked over to it and laid down. He looked at his watch and the iridescent dial told him it was five minutes to one.

He guessed that the cops would only keep up a perimeter for a Peeping Tom for an hour at most, so just to be on the safe side he would stay in the house until at least 2:30 a.m. before making his way back to his car. He relaxed. He would have to postpone having fun in this neighborhood for a month or so since the heat would be on for a while. He smiled when he thought what he would do to "Nan" and her pretty pink nipples when he saw her.

CHAPTER TWELVE

*Oh, what a tangled web we weave,
when first we practice to deceive!*
—Sir Walter Scott

February 1980. I was not a happy camper. The department was changing and not for the better. I had heard other cops bitching, but it hadn't affected me so I figured it was just the usual carping. A squad room has more catty gossip than the break room at a bordello. Anyway, it started affecting me when I came to work one day and there was an envelope in my mailbox from Internal Affairs asking me to report to their third-floor office.

This was my first month back to Watch 3 and I was working with Greg, a rookie who had prior police experience as an LA County Sheriff. He had worked two years at the county jail and Sybil Brand, the county's women's jail. He had been out in Patrol for about four months so I wasn't really training him, but I had to fill out a training sheet on Greg every week. He became irate after he saw one of his ratings and told me so. I had written the following on his training report: "Officer Russo is an excellent recruit. He has a good eye and sees many things on the street that even a seasoned officer might miss. If he has a problem it's that he is too abrupt with citizens. This can be attributed to the fact that Officer Russo worked in county jails for over two years. Since almost everyone in jail is a crook, Officer Russo starts off treating everyone like a crook rather than waiting to see if they prove themselves to be such." It was the events of one night in particular which caused me to make that observation.

It was about 0130 hours (1:30 a.m.) Greg was driving southbound on a residential street south of Anaheim and west of Redondo. Greg saw a little old gentleman who was dressed in a bathrobe and slippers and looked to be in his seventies walking a small white fluffy dog. He pulled to the curb, stopped our car, jumped out, and confronted the old guy. "What are you doing out walking the streets at this time of night?" Greg asked.

"Walking my dog," the man responded.

"No. You're making yourself a target for whatever crook drives by and sees you. What the crook sees is an easy mark. Do you think you're strong enough to beat away a robber who wants to go through your pockets?"

The old man shrugged and said, "The dog has to go."

Greg chewed the guy out for a few more minutes, telling him in so many words how stupid he was to be out in the street at that time of night. I finally came to the gentleman's rescue and told him that we didn't want to have to take a report because he was the victim of a crime and that perhaps this late at night it would be more discreet of him just to let his dog do his thing in his backyard.

When we got back in the car I turned to Greg and asked, "Don't we have enough people out here who hate us without giving someone else a reason to?"

"But that was stupid for the old man to be out there at 1:30 in the morning waiting for some asshole to come by and knock him on his head and take his wallet or house keys," Greg replied.

"You're absolutely right," I said, "but if stupidity were a crime, half this city and all of the city council would be in jail. I agree with everything you told that citizen, but the way you said it could only piss him off. You could have told him essentially the same thing and he would have thanked you for it, but now he thinks that most cops are arrogant, condescending pricks. You've got to learn an essential lesson of good police work. Always start off treating everyone, suspect, victim, witness, or citizen, black, white, brown, yellow, or green, in a friendly, polite manner. An asshole will always mistake kindness for weakness and will show himself to you soon enough, and then you can handle him or her in an appropriate manner. And to everyone else, and everyone who sees it, we'll still be the good guys."

So, back to my first sustained Internal Affairs case that resulted in a finding of misconduct on my part. I received documented counseling which amounts to a "no-no" in your personnel package. I had been to Internal Affairs a few times before and figured this was no big deal. I didn't contact a Police Officers Association representative, thinking that I would first find out what the complaint was for. After the squad meeting, Greg Russo and I went to the third-floor IA office. The sergeant there gave me a copy of the complaint and told me that it was basically about the use of profanity and asked me if I had a representative. I told him that I didn't think I needed a rep. He told Greg that he was just a witness and wouldn't need one.

The arrest that led to this complaint had occurred the week before. I was now working with Greg Russo. He and I had been dispatched to a family dispute on the 800 block of Obispo Avenue. When the wife came to the door, it was obvious she had been battered. Her face and neck were red from being slapped and her left eye was swelling shut. She was still crying, and after she told us her husband had left, we calmed her down, and asked her if she wanted to go to the hospital. When she replied negatively, Greg started taking a report for a misdemeanor wife beating. At that time, any spousal abuse that didn't result in hospitalization was filed as a misdemeanor.

She told Greg that her husband had come home from work drunk and was mad because his dinner wasn't ready. She told him that she was waiting for him to get home so she could find out what he wanted since the last time he had slapped her around his excuse was that she had cooked him something that he didn't like. With that, her husband told her he didn't need an excuse to thump her and started slapping her in the face with his open palm. After he had slapped her three or four times, he threw her to the floor and walked out. She didn't know where he had gone, but his car was still in the driveway so he had to be on foot.

While she finished her story and Greg was getting her vital statistics for the report, the front door opened and in walked her drunken old man. He was a 5'10" White male with long hair and sideburns. He was skinny in a wiry sort of way. He was wearing a Los Angeles Rams jersey that looked like it would have been too big for Jackie Slater. When he saw us, he froze for about twenty seconds, taking in the whole scene, and then his face contorted and he spewed out, "You bitch, ya hadda call out the cops didn't ya?"

As I walked toward him, he told me to mind my own business, that this was his wife, to get out of his house—the usual drunken wife beater rhetoric. I purposefully got right in his face and told him that we were called to his house because he beat his wife, so that made it our business. Then I leaned in right next to his ear and whispered that he was just a "little pussy." My words had their desired effect. The husband tried to push me and take a swing at me, but he was a little too inebriated to accomplish what he intended. His scrawny right hand brushed my left shoulder.

I let his momentum carry him around, then I placed his neck in the crux of my left arm and pulled him back over my hip. I said, a little more loudly than I intended, "You're one tough motherfucker. Why I'll bet you can kick the shit out of 80, maybe 90 percent of the women in Long Beach." I started squeezing his pencil neck between my forearm and bicep. It took longer than usual for the husband to go limp. It is a strange phenomenon, but skinny guys take a lot longer to "choke out" (that is, render unconscious) than the big-necked, weightlifter types. At any rate, after a good thirty seconds, hubby lost consciousness. I put him on the floor and handcuffed him.

Wifey immediately did an about-face and said, "I don't want him arrested. He'll be okay once he sobers up. I won't press charges."

I told her that he wasn't being arrested for beating her, although that would be a secondary charge. He was under arrest for battery on a police officer and I was pressing charges. Greg finished getting the information he needed and tried to tell her that her recalcitrant husband would continue to beat her if she didn't leave him. That was when we heard an infant crying from another room and realized that there was little chance that she would ever testify against the father of her baby. That was the end of it, until the love letter arrived from Internal Affairs.

Greg and I took copies of the complaint to the third-floor coffee shop and started reading.

The wife was the complainant. In addition to the expected bullshit accusations about the "unprovoked brutality" I inflicted on her husband, she accurately quoted what I had said while choking him out. I didn't think this was a major problem necessitating a POA rep. I told Greg we both knew the excessive force beefs were bullshit, and the profanity wasn't a big deal. Then we both went back to Internal Affairs and told our stories, separately and truthfully. When I was done, the Internal Affairs sergeant told me that I could expect a day off for using profanity. I asked when the department started giving days off for that and he responded by saying, "New chief, new policy. The new chief has stated that using profanity is the mark of a poor vocabulary." Just a few months before, the last Chief who had been World War II veterans had retired, and after the City Manager had conducted a search to replace him, we had a new Chief who had been promoted from within. He did have an extensive vocabulary.

At any rate, I wasn't happy about being made the first example of this new discipline policy. (It had technically always been against departmental policy to use profanity while on duty, but the reality was that nobody ever got dinged for it. The reason being that in stressful situations, such as confronting an armed robbery suspect, command and control were deemed more important than community relations. Also, it was thought that the dirtbag might question the officer's command presence if he said, "Sir, please drop your weapon or I will be required to use deadly force to bring this incident to a successful conclusion," rather than the more commonly used phraseology of the time, which was, "Drop the gun, asshole, or we'll fill you so full of lead you could use your pecker for a pencil.") But what could I do? I wasn't going to lie and it was too late anyway. I realized that since the rules of the department's game had changed, I would have to change or be subject to more and frequent "unpaid vacations."

Greg and I discussed this while driving out to our beat. If the department wanted us to have an extensive vocabulary, we would have one. From the most commonly used vulgarities, we came up with a treasure trove of useful and witty phrases. For example, a dumb motherfucker became an "intelligence lacking maternal fornicator," a dirty cocksucker became an "unhygienic fellator," a stupid sonofabitch became "an IQ deficient scion of a cur," a miserable bastard became "paternally ignorant," and a shithead was a "fecal cranium," just to name a few. We had started a politically correct vocabulary before the term "politically correct" had been invented. Even though we laughed ourselves silly with our new terms, we became more and more serious about their application in our police work. I started carrying a full-size dictionary in my kit, and Greg started bringing a thesaurus.

Greg gets credited with coming up with the crowning glory of our new verbal jousting. He said, "When I was working the women's jail for the sheriff's, we had an old lieutenant who told us that we could call the inmates virtually anything we wanted as long as we had what he said was 'plausible deniability.' He told us that meant we had to call them these things indirectly. For instance, don't call someone an asshole, tell them 'You're acting like an asshole.' That way, when they complain, you can honestly tell anyone that you didn't call them that."

So we never told anyone that he was a maternal fornicator. We would state something like, "Sir, you're acting like a maternal fornicator. Please desist." The greatest thing was that it worked beyond our wildest dreams. Try it yourself sometime. Ask some dumb sonofabitch if he's acting like an IQ deficient scion of a cur, and have your tape recorder ready to immortalize his response. It will most likely be "Huh?" or "Say what?" or "Speak English, will ya?"

We liked to tell the other coppers who witnessed our use of our new terms that, "We are able to defuse volatile situations with our witty repartee." Those cops would respond with the standard colloquialism that "You didn't dazzle them with your footwork, you baffled them with your bullshit." True enough, but we didn't admit it to those "paternally ignorant rectums."

We became so proficient at this vocabulary thing that we were able to ad-lib in many situations. At one of the many fraternity parties we were called upon to break up, there was a young coed. She was braced with more than enough alcohol, and her life experience apparently consisted of having been ass-kissed by men in virtually every situation because she was good-looking. She decided to verbally editorialize her opinion of the law enforcement professionals present by stating loudly, "I hate fucking pigs," as she passed Greg and me. She knew she had an audience which was why she spoke with enough volume for all the coeds leaving the party to hear. There were a few guffaws from the crowd.

Armed with our new words and phrases, Greg immediately shot back in an equally loud voice, "Well, darling, perhaps if you switched the object of your affection from the lowly swine to one of the higher echelon equine, you would not only enjoy the carnal act more, but you could also obtain gainful employment in a nearby third world country that offers such entertainment." The obnoxious but beautiful young lady's face went blank and she uttered, "What?"

I responded, "He said that if you change from fucking pigs to mules, you might enjoy screwing more and could get a job in the donkey shows in Tijuana." The otherwise hostile crowd broke into uproarious laughter. The coed turned red, turned back toward Greg and me, and said, "Fuck you."

"Oh, good comeback," I shouted back. "Witty, pithy, and staccato. And the most overused obscene phrase in the world today. Profanity being the first and only weapon of the ignorant, it looks like you have just been unilaterally disarmed in this war of wits." There were a few more titters from the kids and the coed left muttering more profanities to the group she was with.

When speaking with normal citizens, we used normal speech. But, when talking to drunks, gang bangers, most hookers, the arrogant, the obnoxious, the condescending, the prejudiced, the overbearing, or the obstreperous, we found that using our enhanced expressions often defused the situation. I think this was because it caused a confusion that precluded the subject from forming a plan of action to either flee, attack us physically or verbally, or play to the crowd if there was one.

CHAPTER THIRTEEN

Evil enters like a needle and spreads like an oak tree
—Ethiopian Proverb

March 1980. The Skulker's eyes snapped open and he looked at his watch. The radium dial told him it was twelve minutes after four. He was sure that the police perimeter, if one had indeed even been set up, had long since been dispersed. He had rested a little longer than he had wanted but now seemed like the perfect time to leave. It was still earlier than most people awoke to get ready for jobs, yet late enough that he would have already missed the barflies who had come home after the bars closed at 2 a.m., even if they stopped for an early breakfast before heading home.

He gingerly retraced his steps down the hall to the living room, but rather than continuing on to the kitchen, he went to the sliding glass door. He thought that it would be easier to go out that way than to have to re-lock the back kitchen door with the lockpicks. He found the broomstick handle that was sitting in the door channel and lifted it up. He slid the glass door open about 18 inches. He angled the stick in the channel so the one end rested around three feet up on the side of the glass slider opposite the opening and the other end of the broomstick rested on the bottom of the channel. He then crossed the glass door's threshold to the outside and gently pushed the slider closed. The stick slid slowly into the channel and effectively re-locked the sliding glass door.

He treaded lightly across the new subfloor, then slowly walked over the backyard that was uneven with the foundation diggings and normal construction debris. He stopped in the shadow next to the gate and fence. He looked at the neighbors' houses on both sides and didn't see any movement or lights. He listened and didn't hear anything except a dog barking a block or so away. He stood on his tiptoes and looked over the fence. The houses on the other side of the alley appeared dark. He slipped open the gate, passed through, and noiselessly closed it again.

He walked on the dark side of the alley for three blocks, stopping at each street in the shadows, waiting, listening, and looking for any activity prior to crossing the street to the next alley. His car was legally parked about 20 feet from the mouth of the last alley. After the appropriate waiting, listening, and looking period, he walked to it, opened the unlocked door, sat down behind the steering wheel, and eased the door shut. He waited a minute before starting the three-year-old grey Toyota Corolla. He turned on the lights, eased it into gear, and slowly drove out of the area. He was home and in his own bed by 4:30 a.m. His alarm was set for 6:45 a.m., which would give him plenty of time to awaken, shower, and shave before driving to work where he had to clock in at 7:30.

The Skulker closed his eyes. He was more than satisfied with his night's reconnaissance. In his opinion, the fact that one of his prospective "whores" (that's the way he thought of his potential victims) had possibly caught an unrecognizable glimpse of him and probably called the cops hadn't been a defeat. In the worst case, his timeline was merely delayed by a month or two at the most. He wasn't afraid of the police. The cops were stupid, and if he had learned anything from his past mistakes, it was that if he scouted his locations and planned his attacks, developed escape routes and alternate escape routes, the police were not going to be a serious problem. His thoughts drifted to Nan and how she would scream when he clamped onto the nipple he had seen last night. He fell asleep imagining the look of fright and trepidation that would be on her face when she realized what he was going to do to her.

CHAPTER FOURTEEN

Perhaps rape itself is a gesture, a violent repudiation of the female,
in the assertion of maleness that would seem to require nothing
beyond physical gratification of the crudest kind.
The supreme macho gesture—like knocking out an opponent
and standing over his fallen body, gloves raised in triumph
—Joyce Carol Oates

March 1980. The first rape that I became aware of by the cutthroat murdering asshole I later executed occurred in our beat on a night Greg and I were working. It had already been an eventful evening. Right out of the station we had taken a robbery/ attempted murder report in Belmont Heights. Then, later, we went code 7 at a Teriyaki burger joint at Anaheim and Ximeno. We were sitting at a picnic table on the grass next to the burger place when a Volkswagen pulled to the curb on Federation. A big, blond Labrador retriever jumped out of the car, ran over next to our picnic table, and proceeded to shit his brains out right next to us.

Then, after a couple of nothing calls, we were dispatched to a residential neighborhood that was out of our beat, east of the Traffic Circle and north of Los Coyotes Diagonal. The call was a 459 (burglary) now, which meant that it was occurring while the dispatcher was talking to us. The dispatcher told us that the Complaining Party (CP) had heard the suspect scratching at her bedroom window in her backyard. We arrived and parked half a block away with our lights out. Greg and I had already decided that he would go to the front door and meet the CP, and I would go around to the backyard and try to prevent the burglar from escaping over the fence.

We split up at the walkway to the front porch. I veered off to the left where I could see the closed gate and Greg went up to the porch where the woman who called dispatch was standing with the door open just a crack. I reached over the five-foot gate and unlatched it. As quietly as I could I opened the gate and entered the backyard. I kicked a stone over that was next to the gate so that the gate wouldn't slam shut. As I rounded the corner of the house I could hear scratching. With my Kel-Lite flashlight (unlit) in my left hand and my government model 1911 .45 in my right, I moved toward the sound.

The light in the bedroom was on, but was obscured by a plant that was covered with leaves and branches virtually from the ground to the eaves of the house. It was the perfect spot for a burglar to remain hidden while he pried open a window. I didn't know what the burglar was prying with. As I entered the foliage and turned on the flashlight, my finger tightened on the trigger of my gun. As my beam illuminated the inside of the bush, I was unprepared for what I saw.

At the exact same moment my Kel-Lite came on, the window was pushed up from the inside. Before I finished my trigger pull, I realized that Greg was the one who had opened it. Immediately after the window opened, the biggest rat I have ever seen pushed off the side of the windowsill and jumped right at me, bounced off my chest, and scurried away toward the rear fence. When I finally caught my breath, I came to the conclusion that I hadn't fired my gun. I walked over and was admitted to the back door of the house. By then, I had figured out what had happened. The woman in the house had closed her window while preparing to go to bed. In doing so, she had closed the window on the rat's tail and the scratching was the rat trying to extricate himself. When Greg opened the window, the rat's tail was released. It pushed off the window and nearly caused me to have a major heart attack. To this day, I don't know why I didn't fire my gun. When we got back to our car, Greg, the simple shit, or should I say the halfwit fecal pile, couldn't stop laughing.

The night was three-quarters done when the call came in that would eventually cause my dilemma that required me to write this tome. It was about 0020 hours (12:20 a.m.) when we received the 261 (rape) call. It came from a house in an older neighborhood, south of Pacific Coast Highway and west of Redondo in an apartment on Coronado. Mona Ripley was a 34-year-old divorcee who was pretty messed up. It looked like her nose was broken, and she had a scratch on the right side of her face that was oozing blood. It traveled from her right nostril across her cheek and down the side of her neck to her collar bone. In addition, she also had numerous bruises on her face and neck. She was holding her ripped and torn flannel nightgown up against her body, and even with her arms crossed and covering her breasts, we could see the blood stain where her left nipple should be. She was naturally very upset and didn't want to see anyone else, but we called for the paramedics and a lab unit and tried our best to ease her anxiety.

I had been the victim of an armed robbery/kidnapping/ hostage situation when I was a junior in college, working in a fast food joint. As the victim of a violent crime I had been asked to participate in a study on Posttraumatic Stress Disorder by a graduate student name Tak Shimizu at UCLA. We had become pretty good friends and he'd shared the results of the study with me.

Because I had experienced many of the symptoms of PTSD I was able to relate to this woman what she could expect to happen to her, psychologically. First, I told her the rape was not her fault. There was nothing she did to cause this rape. The rape was caused by the miserable lowlife creep. I told her my experience and that I had relived my robbery/kidnap several dozen times and had "what if'd" myself nearly to death thinking that if I had done this or that the crime wouldn't have happened. I related to her how I had had a hard time sleeping for about six months after the crime and that I had nightmares about it and would wake up in a cold sweat. I had lost my appetite, was depressed much of the time, and suffered from insomnia. I told her that my friend Tak said that the theory was that these symptoms were caused by the victim having lost control of the situation. I told her that after speaking with Tak, I understood what was happening to me and I didn't think I was going crazy anymore and I started to feel better. I told her what to expect, psychologically, and if she needed help she should call Tak, and gave her his number.

Before the paramedics arrived, she had calmed down quite a bit and was able to give us the information we needed for the report. She was unable to give much of a suspect description because it was dark and her face was covered much of the time. Over the radio, we put out what little she was able to give us: White male, 5'7" to 5'10", 150 to 180 pounds, possible dark cap, dark shirt, and pants; NFD (no further description).

Mona told us she worked as a dental assistant at an orthodontist's office in Belmont Shore. Choking back tears, she told us that the suspect had bitten her nipples hard enough to make at least one of them bleed. She didn't know how he had gotten into her house because she was sure she had locked and dead-bolted her door. She told us that because of the cold weather, all of her windows were closed and locked. She had been asleep when she was jarred awake by the suspect who was sitting on her and trying to pull down her nightgown. She naturally started struggling and that seemed to excite the suspect. At that point, she made a conscious effort to remain calm and not resist. She said that she didn't fight him again until he started to hurt her, but her fighting seemed to agitate him and he started hurting her more.

After ripping the shoulders of her nightgown while trying to pull it down over her body, the suspect finally realized or decided that he would pull it up and cover her face with it. He then ripped her panties off and pulled down whatever pants he was wearing and attempted to enter her, but was unable to due to a flaccid penis. It was at that time the suspect slapped and backhanded her four or five times about the head and shoulders while calling her a "fucking whore," a "bitch," a "cunt," a "slut," and a "cockteaser," among other not-so-endearing terms. Mona told us that although these slaps hurt, she still maintained her passivity. She also said that the suspect hurt his hand by striking the antique crucifix that she wore on a gold chain around her neck.

The suspect then pulled her nightgown down and saw the crucifix that was then sitting on her face. He grabbed it and pulled it down, breaking the chain. Mona thought that this is when she received her scratch. He then pulled the nightgown back over her face and again tried unsuccessfully to enter her. It was at this point the suspect started to abuse the victim's breasts.

He slapped them a couple of times, then he bent down and bit her right breast. This caused her to scream, although it was muffled somewhat by her nightgown, and she tried to buck the suspect off her body. This seemed to excite him even more and he switched to her left nipple and bit it so hard Mona thought he had bitten it off, causing her to scream again and thrash even more. Mona told us this was when the sick bastard entered her with a full erection.

After around a minute of intercourse, the suspect turned the victim over and had started to sodomize her when he suddenly ejaculated on her back. He then told her that if she called the cops, he would come back and kill her. He told her to keep the nightgown over her head and remain lying on her stomach. She heard him wandering around for a few minutes and then heard her front door open. She never heard the front door close, but Mona waited a few more minutes and then rearranged her nightgown and cautiously made her way to the living room where she saw that her front door was standing open. She closed it and then called the operator who connected her to the police department.

By this time it had been 45 minutes since we had called the paramedics, so we called communications and were advised that the Fire Department was working on a structure fire at a residence in East Long Beach. They had just determined that everyone had gotten out of the house okay and the paramedics, who had been standing by, were in route to our location.

We told Mona that the paramedics were only minutes away and asked her if she could change into a different loose-fitting outfit so the lab unit could take her nightgown, panties, sheets, and the towel she had used to wipe the sperm from her back for evidence. We also asked her to look around to see if anything was missing. After checking for a few minutes, Mona told us that it looked like the suspect had taken her wallet which contained her driver's license and $35. The only other thing she noticed was missing was her grandmother's antique cross and chain that the suspect had ripped from her neck.

The paramedics arrived, walked Mona over to their van, and assisted her into the back of the unit. By this time, several of the more curious neighbors were out and wanting to know what had happened. We talked to all of them, but no one had seen or heard anything. After coordinating with the lab unit as to what we wanted placed into evidence, fingerprinted, and photographed, we told them the victim was at Community Hospital and headed over there.

When we arrived, the ER doctor was just finishing up his exam and initialing several items from the rape kit. He told us what Mona had said about being raped and sodomized. He added that the bruising and the scratch were brutal but minor injuries and that the victim had required twelve stitches in her left breast because the suspect had nearly bitten her nipple off. He told us that this was the most brutal rape he had seen in his six years working in the ER.

We talked to Mona again. We asked her if she had someone to stay with and she said she had contacted a girlfriend who was picking her up. We asked her if she wanted us to get any clothes or anything from her house and she said she would get anything she needed the next day.

Greg and I headed back to the station to file our report, which took us until 0530 (5:30 a.m.). We were both still wound up from the report we filed on the rape and were hungry, so after we changed into our street clothes in the locker room we drove over to the Bonanza, a restaurant on Willow west of Santa Fe. We both ordered the pork chops and eggs and talked about what we would do to the rapist sonofabitch if we ever caught him.

As I was driving home, I was thinking about the fact that all we were able to do for this poor woman was to file paperwork. I hadn't joined the police department to become a glorified pencil-pushing secretary. I knew that more crooks were sent to prison with a pen than with a gun, but with so little to go on, with the suspect attacking in the darkness, with virtually no suspect description and no suspect vehicle description, we were spitting into the wind. I had three sisters and I felt as bad as if one of them had been raped. I had always hated bullies and no one more personified a bully than a rapist. I hated the helpless feeling of not being able to do more for Mona than offer whatever pitiable advice Greg or I could muster.

I was in the dumps as I drove toward my house in Lakewood. When I arrived home, I got out of my car, opened the garage door, and pulled my car in. As I was closing my car door, the door to the house opened and my son, who was three at the time, had the biggest, brightest smile I had ever seen. When he saw me, he started jumping up and down and yelling, "That's my Daddy. My Daddy's home." My spirits suddenly soared. The little pajamaed, blue-eyed towhead was so happy to see me that I couldn't stay down. I ran over to him, picked him up, tossed him in the air, caught him, kissed him, and let him go. Then I ran over to his little sister, who was standing behind him, sucking her thumb and holding her little blanket, and did the same thing to her.

CHAPTER FIFTEEN

When the cops are trying to arrest you,
if you fight back, things go wrong
—Charles Barkley

April 1980. After that first rape, there wasn't another for two months. During that time, Greg and I worked our normal beat most of the time. On occasion, if our shift was short officers, we would have to work in one of the other two areas the PD had divided the city into: the South/Downtown Area or the North/North Town Area. Greg and I were working up in the North on this particular night.

Before I go on, I must mention a little bit about my partner at that time. Greg Russo is about five years younger than I am, and I was impressed with his capabilities as a police officer. My wife and mother-in-law had met Greg one night and told me how good looking he was. I had never given it much thought, but when I mentioned it to him a few days later, he flashed me a condescending, shit-eating grin that I would see thereafter whenever his good looks were mentioned in my presence. It was as if he were saying, "Yeah, I am good looking, you poor ugly bastard."

I, myself, have never been a lady's man. In fact, from puberty on, I had a lot of girls who were my friends, but few who dreamt seriously of me as their romantic Prince Charming. Girls really liked me, but never as a "lover." Not that I didn't have some successes, but I never had girls calling me or asking me out like a couple of my buddies did.

Greg was the opposite. When I worked with him, we did have girls follow us. The dichotomy in our looks was brought home to me, cruelly, one night in North Long Beach. There was a cowboy bar on South Street that had a girls' night once a week. The drinks would be half priced and male dancers would dance for the girls and strip down to their jock straps. This bar also hired off-duty cops as bouncers. (Because of the number of violent and semi-violent incidents that bouncers get involved with, the Department later changed the policy so that it would not issue a work permit for any off-duty job at a location that served liquor.)

We knew a couple of the bouncers who were working that night, and about 2230 hours (10:30 p.m.), we pulled into the parking lot and stopped to talk to the bouncer who was one of our burglary detectives. After conversing with him for about two minutes, the show ended. About a dozen horny, half-drunk 20- to 30-year-old women came pushing out the front door. They were all very attractive and dressed to kill. Three of them walked right over to Greg's window. The best looking in the group bent down, looked Greg right in the eye, and said, "Wow, you're really good looking." She then stuck her head in the window and looked at me, looked back at Greg and said, "Yeah, you're really good looking." Greg turned to me and smiled his shit-eating smile. That was about all I could take. I put the black & white in gear and punched the accelerator. The offending, obnoxious drunken trollop hadn't quite extracted her head from the window and our abrupt departure literally left her spinning.

Considering his good looks, Greg wasn't especially vain, but he was sensitive about a particular look he would get on his face when he was in deep thought. He was right to be sensitive. He would stare off into the distance with a blank look in his eyes and his mouth agape. To say he looked like a village idiot would unjustly disparage village idiots. While in such a reflective state, Greg was unaware of how moronic he looked, but it had been pointed out to him so many times and by a variety of people (and I'm sure some had photos for which I would have paid serious cash) that he knew it was true.

I bid my time and, finally, the circumstances were ideal to wipe the insufferable smile off pretty boy's face. About an hour after the squad meeting, I was driving, patrolling our beat. We were traveling westbound on Anaheim from Redondo when I noticed "Hollywood" Russo had his idiot face on. I stopped at the red light at Obispo. I was in the center lane and a convertible pulled up next to us. I saw that there were two nice, sexy young ladies in the car engaged in light conversation and their car top was down. Perfect. With my moron partner starring off into the sunset, I leaned in front of him and said in my most commanding, stentorian voice, "Well, hello girls!" Before they turned toward us, I leaned back into my seat, grabbed the steering wheel with both hands, and looked straight ahead.

Out of the corner of my eye, I saw both girls turn toward Greg, smile, and say "Hi." Slowly, very slowly, Rainman was coming out of his stupor. When they greeted him he had turned his vacant stare to them and only then realized what was happening. When the light came through the fog, Greg snapped, turned to me, and inquired, "I had that stupid look on my face, didn't I?" Ever the debonair one I leaned forward, smiled, waived to the women, and said, "Hi, ladies." Greg refused to look their way and was telling me out of the side of his mouth to "get the hell out of there." Thinking back to the grinning fool he had been at the cowboy bar, I didn't think he had suffered enough. My revenge was complete when Greg started turning red after the passenger was heard to say, "What's wrong with that drooling fool?" This relatively good natured attack-counterattack game we played continued as long as we worked together.

CHAPTER SIXTEEN

The belief in a supernatural source of evil is not necessary:
men alone are quite capable of every wickedness
—Joseph Conrad

April 1980. The Skulker was ecstatic. He had found his "gold mine." In the east end of Long Beach, there were a lot of single women, divorcees, and co-eds. He preferred divorcees because some of them were pushy and he realized what really turned him on was putting emasculating bitches in their places. The last one had been the best he ever had, and she had been a divorcee. He realized that she had also been so good because she fought as hard as she could. Although he enjoyed the fact that she had resisted, he felt compelled to punish her. He had overcome her fighting and given the bitch exactly what she deserved. It was actually the first time he had tasted blood and he liked it. He could have bitten her anywhere but when he had her trapped in her nightgown, her nipples were staring him in the face and they were the center of his universe for those few precious moments.

He had found the divorcee the month before on his Edison route in the 1700 block of Coronado. She lived in a two-story green apartment with its twin across the courtyard. As he was checking the individual meters on the apartment buildings, he could hear the conversation coming from the laundry room. He took his time listening to the two women talking. Both had obviously just experienced contentious divorces. The more strident of the two was the one called Mona. She told the other one all of the things she had done to her husband after she caught him screwing his secretary.

When Mona had confronted her husband, he'd denied it. Mona told the other woman that her husband then became angry and pushed her to the floor of their home. Mona said her husband had called her a frigid dyke. Mona and the other woman laughed themselves silly when Mona said she told her husband that she just couldn't get turned on by a so-called man who was hung like a stallion hamster. Mona said that her husband stopped his angry fit at that time and she could literally see him shrink and wither away. What had finally sent him running from the room was when she told him that "other women have men who are pythons of passion and I got stuck with the inchworm of love."

At that moment, The Skulker was both repulsed and attracted to the overbearing, pushy, obnoxious Mona. He could feel the humiliation Mona's husband must have felt. He knew that he had to punish her for her emasculating comments to her obviously long-suffering ex-husband. And he did punish her. If she could attack a male's manhood, then he could attack her "womanhood." When he found her bare tits in his face, he knew the perfect revenge. Nothing represented "woman" more than breasts. She had reduced her husband's masculinity by belittling his penis. He would reduce her femininity by ruining her tits. So he bit. Until the bite, he wasn't sure he could get hard enough to penetrate the whore. He was afraid of what she would say about him to other women. But the scream, even muffled by the nightgown, and the struggling while he was biting did the trick. His measly semi-hard-on had turned into a diamond cutter and he gave it to her in the front and back doors. He surprised himself when he enjoyed sodomizing her more than the straight fuck. Then he realized that he was humiliating her just like she had humiliated her husband. He knew that he was hurting her by the way she whimpered. The memory of that was only part of the reason for his ecstasy.

The Independent Press-Telegram had written up the "attack" in their paper, but even more important, he learned that the area he had been working catered to "singles" and that for some reason there were 20 square blocks where there were about twice as many single women as men. He almost wanted to shout "Eureka!" Twenty square blocks was an enormous area. It encompassed a small part of Signal Hill and then went south to 4th Street and from Junipero to east of Redondo. He didn't know for sure, but he thought that this area probably had different police beats in it. He had been told that cops didn't communicate with each other very well, and that would make his "adventures" less dangerous. Signal Hill also had its own police department. He could have his fun in Signal Hill one night and then, a month or so later, he could have some excitement on the far south end of his new fun zone. He figured he could work this area for at least six or eight months minimum before the cops would even begin to catch on. He was getting excited more often now that he had proven to himself he could get away with it.

His notes indicated that he had 10 acceptable single, divorced, or widowed women in those 20 square blocks that he already had more than enough information on to have an "adventure" with. Add to that another 12 or so in the other areas of the city, and he was ecstatic about the future. Life was good and getting better.

His boss at Edison had recommended him for a merit raise and had rated him highly in his performance review. He had gone out a couple of times with his co-workers for beer and pizza after work, and he knew that they considered him to be kind of quiet, but an "all right" guy. He paid his rent on time, early usually, and his elderly landlord liked him for that and because he helped out around the apartment building. He really didn't know his neighbors, but he always smiled and said hello when he saw them. He knew that this would build his reputation as a solid citizen and that would keep him from direct suspicion in case the cops did come sniffing around. In addition, he had chosen his apartment judiciously. It was in the corner of the building and its front door opened into a little walkway that led to the alley. No neighbors, either in his building or the adjoining ones, could see his comings and goings, especially at night.

Not only all of that, but he took precautions. He was patient and he always did his reconnaissance before striking. He carried a pair of dirty gym socks with him. He figured if he was stopped by the cops, he could come up with a believable story as to why he had them (they had dropped out of his workout bag as he got out of the car and had forgotten them in his pocket). But the socks could be used when he didn't want to leave fingerprints. He knew his fingerprints were clean. He had never been arrested for a felony. His juvenile record in Arizona was sealed. He had never been arrested in California. He had never done any military service. But, on the off chance that he might one day get caught, he didn't want to give the cops "the rope to hang him." He had read enough about forensic science that he would throw away the pair of shoes he used on an adventure if he had had to walk through a flowerbed or mud. He constantly changed his brand of shoes and had three pairs of popular brands in reserve. He didn't think he would ever get caught, but if he did, they would have a difficult time convicting him.

Tonight, he was doing a late-night reconnaissance. This was approximately 20 blocks east of where he had committed his first rape almost two months ago. He wasn't going to do anything that night. He was just gathering information on lighting and to see if there were any other activities he should be aware of. It was the middle of May. The nights were getting warmer, so he had on his light jacket, a "Members Only" jacket. Every other man on the street had one. His was dark brown, but not dark enough to look like he was doing anything nefarious. He walked at a normal pace. There was an old man walking his dog across and down the street. The old man was in a bathrobe and slippers, indicating to him that he lived on the block. The old man caught his interest. The man walked slowly down the street past a couple of houses, then turned around and walked back. His little dog stopped and urinated on a fire hydrant. Then the old man went up a walkway to a white stucco house with dark trim. This house was next to a two-story apartment building where one of his higher priority targets lived.

This particular neighborhood, like many in Long Beach, was a combination of single family one-story houses interspersed with one- and two-story apartment buildings. A decade or more before, the City Council had changed the zoning so that apartments could be built in what used to be nice middle class older neighborhoods. This caused congestion, parking problems, and the deterioration of the neighborhoods. It also did something for which The Skulker was very grateful: the people in these areas didn't know each other and as a result didn't talk to each other. This enabled him and other crooks to "case" areas without much fear of citizens calling in anything but the most suspicious activities.

He walked around for another hour. He mapped out shadows, street lights, entryways, and accessible windows in his mind. Then he drove home, wrote out his mental notes, and went to sleep for a few hours before going to work.

CHAPTER SEVENTEEN

Truth exists, only falsehood has to be invented
—Georges Braque

July 1980. Watch 3 officers had to be in the squad room at 1630 hours (4:30 p.m.), so most Watch 3 guys got to the locker room between 4 and 4:15 to change from their civilian clothes into their uniforms. The partner I was working with now was Ted Norris. His father had been a captain on the department and he had a younger brother who had preceded him on the PD. Ted was a fun-loving guy and working with him was a kick. He was all business when that was called for, but in between those situations he was always looking for ways to screw with people, usually me or our overburdened supervisory sergeant, Johnny David.

One afternoon, Dave Ahrens, who worked Watch 2 and normally got off at 1730 hours (5:30 p.m.), was leaving early. He was in the locker room the same time as Ted and me.

As I was changing into my uniform, Ted was getting ready to go take a shower and Dave was changing out of his uniform. There was a bench against the wall that was in close proximity to all of our lockers. I had laid my .45 caliber Colt government model pistol on one end of the bench and Dave had put his 9mm Smith and Wesson at the other end of the bench. I asked Dave how he was getting off duty so early, and he told us that he was on his regular day off and was working a "special," which meant he was working overtime (OT). He told us his sergeant had gotten him the OT assignment. We were more than a little curious, since all overtime assignments were supposed to be handed out on a rotating basis through the Special Events Section. Dave told us that the Deputy Chief of Police had okayed five Patrol Sergeants to hand pick officers to work a month and a half long VIP conference at the Queen Mary. Ted and I knew what that meant. Since our sergeant, David, wasn't picked as one of the "golden boy" sergeants, we wouldn't get any of this prime OT.

I told Dave that I thought that this was chickenshit and he agreed, but smiled and said that he wasn't going to turn down the OT and I wouldn't either if the positions were reversed. I guess I got a little loud about it. I told Dave that even though Boors was a great sergeant to work for, he had a reputation with some of the Brass (the Deputy Chief in particular) as being obnoxious. As a result, if this was the way they were going to hand out OT assignments, the "golden boys," both sergeants and officers, were going to get all of the OT and no one else was going to get any.

While Dave and I were having our rather heated "discussion," Ted fooled around with his locker, grabbed a towel, and headed for the showers. After he left, Dave came over to my side of the bench, grabbed my .45, and said, "You're not getting your gun back until you give me back mine." I was still ticked off thinking about the OT situation and wasn't in the mood for any bullshit from anyone, let alone the messenger of such potentially bad news. I grabbed my gun from Dave.

"I don't have your gun, you simple shit," I croaked. "Go ahead and look in my locker." I stood back from my open locker and let him look.

He checked and then said, "Well, it either had to be you or Norris. What did he do with it?"

"I don't know, and I don't care. I have to go to work." I pushed by Dave and went to the coffee shop to grab a cup of coffee before the squad meeting. When I got to the basement squad room, one of the other Watch 3 cops saw me and told me I'd better give Dave back his weapon or he was going to file a crime report. I told this officer that Dave could file whatever he wanted because I didn't take the "dumbshit's" gun and I wasn't worried.

A few minutes before the squad meeting started, Dave walked in and said, "It's okay, Ted gave me back my gun."

"Well, goody for you, ya zip. I told you I didn't have that piece of crap," I responded.

"Yeah, right," Dave said with a conspiratorial grin. Then he turned and walked out of the squad room.

After the meeting, Ted and I got our black & white and started driving to our beat. I asked Ted why he had taken Dave's gun and where the hell he had hidden it. Ted started giggling like a schoolgirl and said, "Dave thinks you hid it." I asked him why in the world Dave would think that. He said that when Dave and I started arguing, Ted saw Dave look away. That's when he grabbed Dave's pistol and threw it in his (Ted's) locker, closed the door, and went to take his shower.

Ted said that when he came back, Dave was madder than a wet hen and asked Ted if he knew where his gun was. "Is that what

Ed put in my locker?" Ted told Dave as he opened his locker. He reached up on the top shelf, grabbed Dave's gun, and said, "Is this it?"

Dave took his gun and then said, "Yeah, hey thanks, Ted."

I looked incredulously at Ted and said, "Why, you asshole. Now he thinks I took his gun."

"That's right, Ed, and the best part is that no matter what you tell him now, he's still gonna think you hid his gun in my locker. He will not believe that I had anything to do with it." Ted guffawed. He was absolutely right. The next time I saw Dave I tried to tell him what Ted had done and how he'd scammed both Dave and me.

All I got in return was a silly grin and "Sure, Ed, I believe you," said in such a way as to convince me that there was no way he believed me.

Dave's perception was that I took his gun, hid it in my partner's locker, and left him to stew and hunt for it because I was irritated by the fact he was getting OT and I wasn't. His perception was based on certain facts. Only two people could have taken his gun and he was in an argument with one of them (me), which meant I had a motive to screw with him. Further, an alleged eyewitness had so much as told Dave that he had seen me put Dave's gun in Ted's locker. All totally believable. All totally false.

The truth was that I had absolutely nothing to do with the temporary theft of Dave's gun, except as an inadvertent diversion for Ted's skullduggery. You can see how "perception" in this case was not "reality." You can see why I would get upset with those management types who spout such tripe. I have no complaint about them trying to change perceptions. That's logical and positive and worth doing. But to operate under the proposition that perceptions are realities is asinine and causes all kinds of problems. It causes some police administrators who believe and practice such garbage to inflict undue harm on their troops directly and the public indirectly. They sacrifice good officers on the altar of public opinion before a thorough investigation is completed. Just as bad, they'll keep, reduce, or let go unpunished a brutal or less than ethical officer who is an ass-kisser because the "perception" is that he's a "good guy."

This is wrong because police business is about getting the facts and "just the facts, ma'am," as Joe Friday used to say on Dragnet. When we operate on perceptions we're not getting the facts and truth suffers. The precept that "the perception is the reality" has been misinterpreted often and ought to be thrown out of all police management schools.

I feel this way even though I have benefited from this philosophy by not serving time in state prison for murder. The thing is, though, in my case, I think that justice was done by certain people acting as if their perception was the reality. I had a couple of homicide detectives and a deputy chief to thank for perpetrating the perception. But, by doing so, they definitely were enhancing the interests of Justice with a capital "J."

Now, I do not think that police officers, in the ordinary scope of their duties, should or do have a right to take the law into their own hands. Before my incident, I never really did and, since then, I definitely never do. But for every rule, there is the exception that proves that rule, and I think that my case fits into that category.

I'm getting ahead of myself. The sadistic rapist that I killed surely deserved to die, and you will most likely agree. But it wasn't my job to dispense that punishment and I wouldn't have, except for extraordinary circumstances. I thought I was dying.

CHAPTER EIGHTEEN

One of the best things you can do for yourself...
is to learn how to take control of your emotions
—Michael Barbarulo

August 1980. By the time an officer has been out on the bricks for four or five years, his professional personality has pretty much formed. He is an accumulation of his training, the input of his training officers, and his work experience all blended with his base personality that he had when he joined the department. Some cops are forever negative and sour. They may perform their jobs well or even extraordinarily, but they are so cynical and contrary that it's miserable to be around them. Other officers are so passionate about the job, they live it 24/7. These cops usually do a fantastic job for a decade or so and then burn out and take a disability retirement, and they deserve it.

Some in law enforcement associate so closely with victims that they go to pieces after seeing some of the horrors of this job. The toddler who gets hit by a car chasing a ball into a residential street will tear the officer apart. Because of his training, he'll take the fatal accident report professionally, attempt to console the parents, take witness and driver statements, and measure distances. Inside, though, he's thinking how much the dead child reminds him of his own two-year-old boy or girl. He'll suppress these feelings until his shift is over. Then he might get into a crying jag while driving home, or he may drink himself silly with other cops after work. For this kind of officer, after several of these kinds of incidents, he may eat his gun if he hasn't sought out and received help.

Some cops are bullies—brutal, and give the rest of us a bad name. I am not any of those types of officers. My mother tells me that since the day I was born I have had a positive attitude. I don't like bullies, whether they wear a uniform or not. I do feel sympathy for tragedies but, for me, the great advantage of police work is that, after handling such a situation, the police radio will cackle on and send you to some other call that is usually completely different and your mind is occupied stopping two drunks from punching each other's lights out or chasing and arresting a car thief. I guess some cops, by nature, dwell on the tragedies, but not me. I'm always looking forward to the next radio call. I'll remember the tragedies with a twinge of pain, but my thoughts won't linger on them. I'm sure that's why I made it 30 years on the job.

When the rapist started his spree, Ted Norris and I were no longer partners. We had worked together before for about a year, and we were compatible. Ted had a positive attitude like mine; the only difference was that he couldn't quite handle the tragedies as well as I could. He didn't dwell on them, and he wasn't in any danger of eating his gun, but at the scene of some human tragedy, Ted would get antsy. If the suspect who had caused this pain and suffering was at the scene under arrest, I had to watch Ted to make sure that suspect didn't "trip" with his hands cuffed behind his back and fall flat on his face.

We were at Community Hospital about midnight one night filing a non-injury accident report for another unit that had arrested a drunk driver. The graveyard unit that worked our beat on that shift came into the little reporting room that the hospital had set aside for police next to the Emergency Room.

The two cops were good guys (for graveyard cops, who are all crazy), who had acquired the nickname of "Medical Supply Company" or "MSC" for short. Their names were, crazy enough, Johnson and Johnson. I was finishing writing up my report, and Ted was on the phone getting me a report number, when Mack Johnson came into the room and sat at the only other desk that was free. As Ted hung up, he asked Mack what they had going because he was not his usual happy-go-lucky self. Mack told him that he and Stan had just arrested a stepfather who had abused his 16-month-old daughter by putting her under a scalding hot water faucet because she kept crying. Ted told Mack, "Don't let me see the kid, whatever you do, don't let me see her. It'll drive me nuts."

I was done with my report, and told Ted that I was going to the john and would meet him at our car. When I came out the Emergency Room doors a few minutes later, I saw Ted was at the back door of a police car with a handcuffed suspect by the throat, choking the piss out of him. Stan was trying to pull Ted's hands from the man's throat. I went over to help. We freed the suspect and I pulled Ted to our car.

"I told your partner not to let me see the kid. Man, I can't stand it," Ted yelled over his shoulder. Stan was brushing off the suspect and putting him back in the car.

"I'm sorry, Ted. I didn't know," said Stan. To the child abuser he said, "Now you know how it feels to get attacked when you're totally helpless, asshole."

After putting Ted in our car, I walked over to Stan and asked him what he was going to do. He told me not to worry, that he and Mack would "cover it." He said, "Norris just did what Mack and I wanted to do to this motherfucker ourselves."

Another time Ted and I were dispatched on a death notification for a 22-year-old girl who was killed in a traffic accident on the freeway. We were sent to tell the parents. The California Highway Patrol would normally make such a notification when the death happened on the freeway, but some generous new Communications Sergeant had told them we would do it if they didn't have any units available. Ted was arguing with the Communications Operator that the CHP should handle it when the new sergeant got on the radio and ordered us to make the notification.

Since I was driving, Ted was supposed to be the one to tell the parents, but he told me, "I can't do those. I just can't make death notifications. You're going to have to tell the parents." No cop likes to make those notices and I told him that he was up and to do his job. (I was the senior officer.) Ted told me he would get tongue-tied and didn't know what to say. I countered that when we got to the parents' house, whoever saw or contacted anyone inside or outside the house first would make the death notice. Ted agreed.

When we arrived at the house, I parked the car in front of the house next door and we got out of the black & white. At the front door, I knocked and rang the doorbell. After a moment or two with no response, I turned to Ted and said, "Well, buddy, I guess you just dodged a bullet."

Ted, who wasn't very anxious to make the notification, surprised me a little when he said, "There's lights on in the back, let me look over the fence." He walked up the six-foot white wood gate across the driveway, and as he was stretching to see over it, a man about 60 years old in blue shorts, a white T-shirt, and a barbecue apron started walking up the steps to the back door. He spotted Ted and said, "What can I do for you, officer?"

Ted said, "Can you go to the front door, my partner has something he has to tell you."

I was more than a little peeved. The man's wife had heard her husband's conversation with Ted and followed her husband into the house. When Ted rejoined me on the front porch, I whispered, "You asshole, why didn't you just open the gate and we could have told them on their patio?"

Ted mumbled that he wasn't any good at this (as if anybody was), and that I would do it better. Ted clammed up when the father opened the door. Then I asked him his name just to confirm that the Chippies hadn't screwed up the name and/or the address. I asked if we could come in. The father stood aside and motioned us in. I asked the mother and father to please sit down and said that I had some bad news that their daughter, Sandra, had been in a very bad car accident. The mother immediately asked, "Is she going to live?"

"No, ma'am. As a matter of fact, she has passed away." After a pause, I asked, "Is there anything we can do for you? Can we get a neighbor or call a relative to sit with you?"

The shock to the parents was obvious. Their emotions hadn't registered yet and they just sat there with uncomprehending looks on their faces. At this point, something kicked in for Ted and he walked over to the woman, bent down, grabbed her hand, and gently said, "Ma'am, can I get you a glass of water or milk? Would you like me to start a pot of coffee or anything?"

The mother looked at Ted blankly and then said, "I guess we better start some coffee. We'll have to call Sandy's sister and brothers so it will be a long night." She arose from her seat next to her husband on the sofa and started for the kitchen. Ted said that he would help and followed her.

The father sat there, staring off into the distance for a few minutes. Then he looked over at me and said, "You know, you raise your kids from diapers to grade school to junior high and high school, and then they go to college. They think they're mature adults but to you they're still your babies. Sandy was our last one here. She graduated from Long Beach State in June. She got a job last month working for a CPA and he really liked her and was going to send her back to school next semester. She was moving into her own apartment the day after tomorrow in Lakewood. She was just starting life and now it's over. Sandy was our youngest and we spoiled her. And for what.... for what?"

I could see the tears welling in his eyes. He buried his face in his hands. I let him cry for a while. When he had composed himself somewhat, I told him, "Sir, I don't know any words that can console you after such a loss. I don't think there are any. I guess from what your wife said, Sandy had a sister and some brothers, and all I can hope for is that they'll be some comfort for you and your wife as you'll be for them. If you'd like, I could start calling them or we could have other police units go to their houses and notify them."

"No, Officer. I think it would be better if I told them myself. Can you dial the numbers for me? I'm a little shaky right now."

My heart ached for the old guy, who looked like he had aged 10 years since we had first seen him in the backyard. After I had dialed and the father had spoken to the daughter and two brothers, Ted and the mother came out of the kitchen. Ted told the parents that we would stay with them until some of Sandy's siblings arrived. They told us all about their daughter and showed us a recent portrait-sized photograph of her. She had long, black hair and startlingly piercing blue eyes.

The sister and one of the brothers arrived at the same time. We left the family to console each other and commiserate without us.

Back in our car, I told Ted that I hated making death notices and he said, "So do I, but we did a good job back there." Ted's statement was confirmed about a month later when we were told by our Sergeant that the parents had sent the chief a letter of commendation for how "sensitive and well these officers handled a difficult situation involving the death of their daughter." I told Ted that he impressed me with the way he came back after a shaky start and that he had done a great job helping the mother. He told me that once she started the coffee maker, she had collapsed into his arms and sobbed for about five minutes. Ted said he just hugged her and patted her back and teared up a little himself. When she saw Ted's tears, she thanked him "for caring."

A lot of the public think that cops are heartless bastards who don't give a damn about anyone but themselves and other cops. This certainly isn't true. When an officer has to make a death notification, the first thing he thinks about is his own family. The good cops think about how to break such devastating news in a way they would prefer to have such terrible information passed along to them if they were being notified of a family tragedy.

CHAPTER NINETEEN

Rationalization is a process of not perceiving reality,
but of attempting to make reality fit one's emotions
—Ayn Rand

October 1980. It was the whore's own fault. The Skulker was working his job, checking the meters in North Long Beach, which was out of his usual area, because another meter reader had called in sick. Although he appeared outwardly calm, his mind was racing. He had killed a small child and a whore the night before. It was the whore's fault. She had never had a child with her when he did his scouts. He still couldn't figure out why the child was in the house. He didn't know how seriously he had hurt the little girl at first because the child had snuck up and scared him while he was in the middle of his rape. He had reached back with the razor he had taken to using on his adventures, and slashed at the noise behind him. This had panicked him, and caused him to overreact. If the bitch hadn't been babysitting or whatever she was doing with a small child sleeping over in her house, he wouldn't have been forced to kill the kid.

He had jumped off the bitch and kicked the child. He didn't know if it was a boy or a girl until later. That was when the whore pulled her nightgown from her head and started screaming not to hurt "the baby." Normally, the screaming would turn him on, but he was afraid that this scream would escape the house and send the neighbors to their phones. Somehow, the woman, who up until then had been fighting but was easily overcome, developed superhuman strength. She kicked him in the chest and sent him sprawling across the room. He couldn't breathe and he could barely see. She leaped on him and started to pummel him with her closed, sharp-knuckled fists. The more the child whimpered, the more her blows rained down on him. All he could do was lash out with the razor. He thought that he had hit her in the neck once when suddenly she slowed down. He was drenched with a hot sticky liquid that he figured was blood.

He was able to knock her off of him and slash the other side of her neck. She was still writhing under him and that excited him again. He was about to finish what he had come for when he realized that she was still. He couldn't feel her breathing and knew what that meant. The thought that he was now a murderer was sobering. It was then that he heard the child. He grabbed at the sound. By then his night vision had returned. He realized that the whimpering child in his grasp was a girl. He thought to himself that he wasn't one of those perverted pedophiles, but what was he going to do with this kid? Just a couple of days before he had read of a murderer who was convicted in part because of the testimony of a small child.

He grabbed a pillow that had fallen off the bed during the struggle and held it over the little girl's face. It took a lot longer than he expected. He checked every couple of minutes. Finally, after what seemed to him like an eternity, when he took the pillow off the child's face, she was not breathing. He was covered with blood; his clothes were soaked with it. Most of it was from the woman, where he had apparently hit the carotid artery on one side; some of it was from the little girl when he had reached back and slashed her above her hairline. Her long, blonde hair was matted with blood. Then he realized that some of the blood was his own. He felt the oozing from a small cut above his left eye. His face felt swollen from where the whore had hit him several times after she had kicked the wind out of him.

He cautiously approached the bedroom window that faced the house next door and looked through the crack in the curtains. He didn't know how much noise they had made. He remembered the woman had screamed. But the window was closed and the house next door was dark. He went to the other side of the house and saw that the house on that side was also dark. Then he looked out the front and back windows to see that the houses across the street and the houses beyond the back fence were also dark. He figured he had enough time to clean up.

He willed himself to slow down his breathing. He found the bathroom because it had a small nightlight in the wall socket next to the sink. Even in the shadows of the nightlight in the mirror, he could see that his face looked like he had been in a fight. The worst thing though was the deep cuts on his left hand and the scratches on his arms. The razor had cut 2 three-inch slashes, one on the back of his left hand and one on his palm.

He hadn't realized during the struggle that he had done that to himself.

He had to figure out how to get rid of all of the blood on his clothes. He had to clean himself up so that if he was seen he wouldn't look like he had just been in a fight. He looked at his watch. 1:23 a.m. He thought that since none of the neighbors had been disturbed, he could wash his clothes and perform a little first aid on himself and leave in an hour. He was thinking that the time the bars closed at 2 a.m. would be the perfect time to walk to his car about three blocks away. The cops would be busy either arresting the drunks leaving those bars or taking accident reports from the drunk drivers who had just finished their "last call" drinks.

He was wearing dark clothes, so he just had to get the blood out and get them semi-dry before leaving the house. He found the washer and dryer with his little penlight and stripped down to his skivvies. Then he noticed that his boxer shorts were sticky with blood that had soaked through his sweatpants, so he took them off and put all of his clothes in the washing machine. As an afterthought, he took his running shoes and socks that he had set aside and threw them in the washer too. In the cabinet above the washer, he found some soap and put a handful in the machine and started it. A quick wash and spin dry would only take 10 minutes according to the dial. He started the machine and found the bathroom.

With the help of a nightlight he turned on the water in the shower and waited for it to get warm. While he was waiting, he searched the medicine cabinet and found bandages, disinfectant, gauze, and Vaseline. On a shelf next to the sink, he found the bitch's makeup and thought he could use some of it on his face to cover some of the bruising that was starting to show.

He tested the water from the shower and then adjusted it to a moderate temperature. In the glow of the nightlight, he took a very quick yet thorough shower and washed his hair. He dried off with a large towel that was on a hook on the door. He then carefully walked back to the laundry room and pulled his clothes out of the washer, put them in the dryer, and turned it on.

He walked back to the bathroom and then started to examine his cuts. None were very deep and the bleeding had stopped while he was showering. He put some disinfectant on each cut and winced at the stinging sensation. He patted the excess off with tissues he'd found on a box sitting on the toilet tank. He then put a little Vaseline on each cut to prevent any additional bleeding. He looked at his left eye and saw that it was swollen. The fact that it was cut was probably some good luck since it most likely wouldn't turn into a black eye. But it was pretty deep and jagged so, after he found some Q-tips, he disinfected it as best he could and then made and put a couple of small butterfly bandages over the wound.

Then he noticed a bad bruise on his right cheek. He took the pancake makeup out of the little zippered bag from the shelf. He thought it best if he put the makeup on after he put his clothes back on. With his penlight, he carefully walked to the laundry room, avoiding the blood near the bedroom that contained the two bodies. His clothes were still slightly damp but were passable. He put them back on. It felt a little clammy, but it wasn't too bad. The worst thing was that his running shoes were still fairly waterlogged, but there was nothing he could do about that. He carefully walked back to the bathroom and, with the help of the penlight, applied the pancake makeup over his bruised face. He couldn't get it right and was getting frustrated when he realized it didn't have to be perfect at night. All he was doing was walking to his car and the streetlights wouldn't be enough to notice any injuries even if he walked right passed someone on the street. So he blended it into his skin as best he could and looked around to see what he should take with him.

He found a small gym bag in the hall closet. He put the towel, the makeup bag, and the washcloth he had used in the shower in the bag. It suddenly came to him that he had left the straight razor in the bedroom with his victims. It might have his prints on it and even some of his own blood. With penlight in hand, he stepped lightly into the bedroom. Shining the light around he saw it, apparently where he had dropped it, on the floor next to the bitch's body.

Unfortunately, a pool of blood had flowed over and around it. He had been wearing latex gloves at the start of his adventure but they had come off in the struggle, maybe when he cut himself. From what he had learned about fingerprints from his research, liquid destroyed fingerprints. Blood was a liquid so he felt safe in assuming that his fingerprints had been rendered useless. Anyway, he had no record so he didn't see how it would matter even if he did leave his fingerprints; that is, unless he ever got caught. And he planned to never let that happen.

As he put everything he thought could be used as evidence against him in the gym bag, he thought of the two murders he had just committed. He didn't feel bad at all; he thought that the asshole woman had brought it on herself for fighting back the way she did and for somehow having a little girl in the house with her. He was curious as to how the child came to be at the house and who she was, but there was no remorse. He knew he would have felt incredibly worse if he had hit and killed a dog that ran in front of his car. He had always liked dogs.

He thought about the best way to leave: through the front or back door. If the light on the front porch had been on, he would have left through the back. He didn't like leaving through the backyard most times though unless there was an alley. Gates were hard to open quietly and they were usually near neighbors' bedrooms. But he had taken care of the porch light while working the neighborhood for Edison the week before. He had known the whore wasn't home and so, after reading her meter at the side of her house, he went to the front door and knocked. While he waited for an answer that he knew wouldn't come, he scanned the area. There were no cars and no one walking the street at 10:30 in the morning on a weekday. In addition, he didn't see any nosy neighbors peeking through their curtains. He reached up and twisted the bulb until it came loose and then he put a small paper gum wrapper that he had wadded up into the socket and replaced the bulb. With the paper wrapper blocking the connection the light wouldn't go on.

A nighttime scouting run the previous night had confirmed that the porch light wasn't on.

He went out the front door, which he closed softly behind him, and walked down the street toward where he had parked his car. After passing a couple of houses, he started an even-paced jog. It was a natural-looking thing with him in his sweats and running shoes and carrying a gym bag. He turned onto the next block and found his car parked where he had left it, in the shadow of a large willow tree. He threw the gym bag on the passenger seat and retrieved his keys from under the driver's seat. He started the car and drove toward home. On the way, he drove to the back of a supermarket, got out of his car, and lifted the lid on the Dumpster. He emptied the gym bag into it, and put the gym bag itself into the adjoining Dumpster, then got back in his car and drove home.

Now he was plagued with doubts. First, he had to fake a little accident in the locker room at work. He had arrived early and had taken a mop and pail out of the custodian's closet and splashed some water on the floor in the men's room by the sink. He had waited until one of the other employees came in and then faked a slip and fall into the mirror above the sinks. He pulled the scab off the wound above his eye and there was enough blood to make it look believable.

Rudy, a fellow meter reader who had heard the "slip and fall," was trying to get him to sue Edison. His supervisor was pleased when he said that it was no big thing. When his supervisor had bandaged the wound, he had noticed the bruised cheek, but assumed it had all happened in the men's locker room.

He had been upset when his supervisor told him he wouldn't be working his regular area that day. His supervisor thought he was doing him a favor by giving him the easier route when a co-worker had called in sick so he didn't want to make too much of a stink. Even if he wasn't scheduled to work in the whore's neighborhood, he could still drive by and see if anyone had found the bodies yet. If the police were there, he could pretend to read the meters on the block and might be able to find something out. But now he would have to wait until next week, this being Friday. The bad part about this whole mess was that he hadn't really been satisfied by last night's adventure.

CHAPTER TWENTY

A goal without a plan is just a wish
—Antoine de Saint-Exupéry

October 1980. When Ted and I returned back to work on Tuesday, we already knew of the murders in our beat. It had hit the Press-Telegram on Sunday. A woman, Sara Jane Toomey, 27, and her niece, Alice Wilson, aged 3, were found dead by the child's parents who had just returned home from a three-day cruise to Mexico. Sara had volunteered to babysit Alice while her sister and brother-in-law were on the cruise for their fifth anniversary. Sara and Alice were supposed to pick up the parents in San Pedro on Saturday, and when they didn't show up they caught a cab to Sara's house. The husband, who was a fireman in Riverside, found the front door unlocked and walked in. When he saw the blood in the hallway, he pushed his wife back outside and went to the next-door neighbor's house to have her call the police. It was front page on Sunday's newspaper and that, in conjunction with the Ridley rape, had me concerned.

After the squad meeting, Ted and I went to the third floor Homicide office. I told Terry Hensen that the murders had occurred in my beat and asked him what detectives were assigned to the case. He told me facetiously that he and his partner Bob Boyd were the "lucky ones." No cop enjoys working on a case of a murdered child, although we do enjoy arresting and convicting killers for capital offenses.

Terry asked if we had noticed anything out of the ordinary happening in our beat lately. Ted told him that he thought there were a few more prowler calls than normal. I told him that we had had a rape in a downstairs apartment not too far from where these murders had been committed, maybe six blocks. I mentioned that there had been no forced entry on the rape, and the victim was sure she had locked her front and only door. Terry told us that he would know for sure when the lab results came back, but his partner thought this looked like a rape that had gone bad. Terry said that the suspect had left very little usable evidence behind and asked us to keep an eye out for anything that might appear strange in our beat.

Terry told us what we were already thinking, that we should start stopping and talking, and do file shakes (field interrogation cards) on any man out in a residential area after dark.

I told Ted that we should go up and talk to some of the Sex Crimes detectives on the off chance that the Ripley rape and the homicides were connected.

In Sex Crimes, the crusty old sergeant, Doug Croy, asked me, "What the hell are you doing up here ruining my day?"

I told him that I thought the double homicide might be related to Mona Ridley's rape. Sergeant Croy told me that he had gone out to the apartment and looked around for more evidence. He had a good look at the door lock. He hadn't noticed any unusual scratches on the locks, but he said a good lockpick man wouldn't leave any. He said his partner, Dick Robins, was looking at prior tenants and they had already eliminated the landlord from the list of suspects. Croy told us that he would look into what kind of a lock was on the door to the house where the double homicide had been committed. If they were the same type of lock as on Mona Ripley's apartment, the suspect, if he was the same suspect, might have a master key for that type of lock. He told me that when we were shaking guys down we should look for lockpicks and/or master keys.

When I went to the back steps of the police building, Ted was waiting with one of the older black & whites. Unless you were one of the first seven or eight officers out of the squad room, you had to work your shift in one of the older, used and abused police cars. Some cops took great care of the cars, but most of us figured the trustees who worked in the jail would clean them up at the end of shift. Our cars certainly did get abused. Most of them were driven 20 or more hours a day. They were puked in, shit in, pissed in, and filled with all sorts of smelly food bags containing leftover onion rings, hamburgers, hot dogs, fish sandwiches, and other miscellaneous fast food items.

When the squad meetings were over, the race was on to get one of the newer cars. Some years the city experimented with new types of police cars. One year, they bought a few cars with diesel engines in an attempt to save money on gas. These cars were uniformly hated by cops. We were used to fast Dodges with big engines, and although the diesels were all right after they got going, they went from zero to sixty in about a half an hour.

Anyway, the older car we had today wasn't too bad and, as we took off to our beat, I told Ted what Doug had said.

We planned to meet up with Johnson & Johnson, who covered our beat on our days off. (They had recently transferred to Afternoons from graveyard.) We thought that on the one day a week we worked in conjunction, if we were both in the same beat, we could work out a pattern and schedule for stopping and shaking suspicious men.

The main problem was that our beat was the largest in the city. Beat 2C9 went from Ocean to Pacific Coast Highway and from Cherry to Ximeno. A few years later, the department would divide that area into two units, but back then it was just one and was usually patrolled by one car. It was also the busiest beat in the city as far as calls for service, which didn't leave much time for what today is called "proactive" police work.

Our beat was bordered on the easternmost part of Area One or the downtown area, which was also almost always busy. However, to the east there were several units that weren't that busy. Belmont Shore had a lot of bars/night clubs but usually not that many calls, and the rest of East Long Beach was known as "Sleepy Hollow," since it was primarily made up of residential neighborhoods.

We went to the units that were out with us on the east end of town and asked them if they could cover our beat from midnight to end of Watch (EOW) so we could be free to stop and shake anyone out walking or driving aimlessly in our beat. We met these units between calls or when we heard they were code 7 or filing a report at Community Hospital. They were all agreeable except the two oldest guys, Mavar and Colbrook, who worked beat 14. They thought it was too far for them to come out. When we told them that they would only be called if the other units were all out of service they finally agreed, but they wanted us to let them eat in one of our spots on the nights we worked together.

Mavar and Colbrook were slugs working the slowest beat in the city. We thought their offer over for about 30 seconds and told them "no deal." We had five units who said they would watch our beat for a couple of hours and we didn't need them. In addition, I was planning to call Bonnie Garcia, the radio dispatcher for our area, to tell her what we were planning so she would route our calls to the other units.

Mavar and Colbrook kind of pissed us off so when I called Bonnie, I also told her what those two slugs had said. Bonnie told me she would take care of them and I had no doubt that they would receive the bulk of all of the crappiest calls in East Long Beach for a couple of nights. I loved Bonnie.

Later that night, when the graveyard units hit the bricks, we met with our corresponding Watch one unit, my old graveyard partner, John Transom, and his current partner, Jace Eddings, who were working 2 Adam 9. We told them what we were doing. They said they would arrange things on their shift to help us. Over coffee at Hof's Hut on Bellflower. We made up a tentative schedule for canvassing our beat, with Ted and I starting from the south end and working north, and John and Jace starting in the north. They also agreed to contact Signal Hill PD and advise them about the rapes and the possible connections with the murders and to see if they had anything similar happen in their city. (John and his partner met with us later and told us that Signal Hill had a rape that had occurred near their border with us and that there had been no forced entry.)

We started at midnight that same night and we stopped, talked to, and filed 12 shake cards. I didn't think we had any good possible suspects for the rape/murders, but I figured a couple of the guys we shook down were good for auto burgs in our beat. I could see that a bonus to our proactivity was going to be fewer crimes committed between 0000 and 0200 hours (midnight and two in the morning).

Ted thought that one of the guys we stopped might be good as a Peeping Tom because he was dressed in dark sweats. He claimed he was just out jogging and he might have been. He lived about two miles away from where we stopped him. He said that he often jogged in the late evenings and early morning because it was cooler and there was a lot less traffic. We told him he should put on light-colored clothing or someone might mistake him for a burglar and shoot him. But he had legitimate ID and a job and had been slightly winded when we stopped him. He was friendly and cooperative, so we filed our shake card and let him jog on.

I hand-copied each shake card. Then, when we got to the station, I copied them again (both sides) on the Xerox machine. I sent the Xeroxed copies to Terry Hansen in Homicide and turned in one set of the handwritten copies to reporting. I then put the second set of cards in a small plastic file box we had purchased at Sav-On along with the alphabetical separation cards. By that time, it was 0230 hours (2:30 a.m.) so I didn't alphabetize the cards. I just put them in my locker with my kit, changed clothes, and went home.

On our first day back from our weekend, we met with Johnson and Johnson who at that time worked 2C9. I'd left a note for them before we went on our days off. Since this was our overlap day, we wanted to find out if they had gotten my note and what they were doing. They said they'd been hitting the FIs (Field Interrogations) hard too. We figured between Johnson & Johnson, Transom and Eddings, and us, we had turned in a total of forty to fifty FIs in the six days since we had started targeting areas in our beat.

Later that night we got hold of John and Jace to exchange information. They told us that they had contacted their overlap unit, Chrystie and Morgan, and they were hot to do something to catch the rapist/murder. Transom told us that Morgan, who had six daughters, was especially anxious to get the sonofabitch.

None of us, though, thought that we had stopped and FI'd the suspect yet, except for Ted who said that he just had a feeling about the jogger we had stopped and shook who was wearing black sweats. Ted told us that he really wasn't sure that this guy was the murderer, but that the guy was too cooperative. Ted said, "I just got the feeling talking to him that he was up to no good and that he was a peeper. He had righteous ID but, like I said, he was just too helpful with his information."

I dug out our little card file, and Ted found the guy's card so we could share the information on this suspect with the other units. His name was Omar Parkinson. He lived at 2131 East 5th Street, apartment 5. He gave his business address as 100 Long Beach Boulevard and his occupation was a meter reader for Edison. He was a White male, 5'9", and weighed 160 pounds. He had brown hair, brown eyes, and no facial hair. All in all a pretty ordinary looking guy in every aspect.

The other units liked our file method but thought it was too much trouble to hand copy each FI They agreed to Xerox all of their FIs before turning them in so that we could compare them once a week to see if any of the same guys kept showing up. By midnight we had split up and were each covering a different area of our beat. Ted and I were only able to spot three guys to FI before End of Watch. We were sure that the extra attention was cutting the crime rate in our beat, which was good, but we still wanted to catch the rapist-murderer-baby-killer.

The next night we FI'd only two possible suspects, the night after that another two, and on our last work night of the week we FI'd five. I didn't know if this would work but it had a better chance than just going about our business as usual. You never really know about catching bad guys. Most of the times with a known suspect or a suspect who has a regular modus operandi (M.O.), stakeouts and surveillances will get him. But, with something like this, it can be something innocuous like a parking ticket, the suspect getting arrested for a different crime, or just pure dumb luck that gets the guy caught. Anyway, doing something was better than doing nothing.

CHAPTER TWENTY-ONE

In order to escape accountability for his crimes,
the perpetrator does everything in his power to promote forgetting.
Secrecy and silence are the perpetrator's first line of defense
—Judith Lewis Herman

October 1980. The Skulker knew what he had to do. It was simple and he could do it easily. He just had to lie low for a few months as far as having his fun was concerned. He didn't want to, but he knew he had to. He had been stopped and his information had been obtained by the cops. He had committed no crime that night and had nothing incriminating on him when the cops stopped him, but they now had his vital statistics. He was just doing a night reconnaissance, so he didn't have any gloves or lockpicks or a knife; he was clean, which was why he had let them stop him. He wasn't even sure that they had seen him, but rather than chance running away, which brought the unlikely prospect of getting caught and surely having the finger of suspicion pointed at him, he had submitted to the stop.

He had seen the cops at about the same time he thought they had seen him. One of the few cars out after midnight was passing on one of the residential streets and he had slowed down his walk to let the car pass as he crossed the street. He had seen what he thought was a cop car about three blocks down. He thought he could probably avoid them, but there was no danger even if they did stop him, so when the car passed, he started a little jog like he had been jogging all along. He had gone about two blocks when the cop car pulled up next to him and the cops asked him to stop.

He complied and tried to be as charming as he could be. He willed himself to look honest and cooperated with the cops in everything they asked. He kept a small wallet that contained his driver's license with him when he reconnoitered so that if he was stopped, they couldn't find a reason to arrest him. The two cops talked to him and he noticed that the one who took his ID and ran him for warrants on the police radio also filled out a card with all of his pertinent information. That gave him a start, but the more he thought about it the less a concern it became. They had his name and address and date of birth and work address, and when he asked the cop writing on the card what he was doing, the cop told him that there had been a lot of car burglaries in the area and he was wearing dark sweats and jogging at this time of night, which made him look suspicious. He told them that he jogged at night because quite a bit of the time he had insomnia, and it was always cooler at night anyway and there was less traffic. One cop seemed to buy this explanation, but the other one gave him a sarcastic look like he didn't buy it at all. The skeptical cop told him that he should be wearing something white at night if he was jogging so that he wouldn't get run over by a car or shot as a burglar. He told the cops that from now on he would.

He knew what he had to do to throw suspicion off himself. He'd thought about it all the way home. First, he would not have any more adventures for a few months. Second, he would start a routine of night jogging in conjunction with his reconnaissance. (He may have to postpone his adventures, but when he started up again he would be prepared.) He would try to make himself seen by the cops as often as possible, wearing a white sweatshirt or T-shirt, late at night. He figured that familiarity assuaged suspicion. He would also start looking for a new apartment that met his strict criteria. He had seen a few while he was reading meters that might fit his needs. Come to think of it, there were a few houses that had garage apartments behind the main house and almost all could be accessed from the alleys. As a matter of fact, he had seen a rear house for rent that seemed to meet his needs on the three- or four-hundred block of Newport.

He knew that the State of California required people to make notification of any address changes with the Department of Motor Vehicles within two weeks or a month or something like that, but he didn't plan on making that notification. If or when he was stopped by the cops again, he would show them his driver's license with his old address, and if they ever started looking for him they would start there, buying him some time, hopefully.

He jogged home, where he sat down at his dinette table and wrote out his instructions to himself in his own shorthand. The next day, he would try to find a rear house for rent and if that didn't work out, perhaps he would look at some garage apartments. He might even find a good spot while he was reading meters.

He also started thinking about what would have happened if he had been out on one of his adventures that night. The cops would have probably found his gloves and knife and maybe his lockpicks. He was in a quandary. He had to have those things in order to have a successful adventure, but he couldn't think of a better way to hide them. His jacket had special hidden pockets for the picks, but how could you hide latex gloves? Or a knife? At the very least, if he were caught with the gloves, he would look guilty of something and would be taken into custody. If that happened they would undoubtedly find the lockpicks. They would start looking at him for other crimes and maybe for one of the rapes or, possibly, the murders.

Well, since he wasn't going out for any adventures for a while, he had plenty of time to find a solution. He had always thought that he didn't want to carry a gun, but really, what did he have to lose? If the cops got too close when he started back to his adventures, he would have a piece with him to even things out with them. A gun would have an added advantage of putting fear into the whores who were the objects of his adventures.

He knew a little about guns. One of his mother's "friends" while growing up was a hunter and had taken him wild boar hunting. He had let The Skulker use a Government Model 1911 .45 caliber handgun. It had quite a kick when he was 13 years old, but now he figured he could handle it. Thinking about it a little more, though, he realized that he would need something a little less bulky. He knew the difference between a semiautomatic and a revolver and thought that a little .22 or .25 caliber semiauto would do the trick. He would read up on it at the library before making a decision.

The next day after work, he went to the downtown library and started looking up magazine and newspaper articles on handguns and ammunition in the reference section. The irony that he had to park his car in the parking structure across the street from the police station wasn't lost on him. He stayed in the library until closing and came back the next day after work. On Saturday, he spent five more hours there.

The result of his research was that the best bet for what he wanted a gun for was a .22, .25 or .380 caliber semiautomatic handgun that could hold at least six bullets. What his research suggested (but he couldn't confirm) was that the smaller caliber bullet could penetrate the human body, but did extensive damage by bouncing around off of bones. Of course, you couldn't match the knockdown power of a .45, but they didn't make too many small concealable .45s. He thought that if he were forced to use the gun, it would be at close range and he could try a head or gut shot to disable a cop.

He had to find a way to purchase the gun that could not be traced to him. He knew that Arizona had much more liberal laws on the sale and registration of handguns than California. He didn't know exactly what the laws were in California but figured he didn't want to go to a gun store in order to buy one. He had seen an ad about a gun show in Anaheim but didn't want to buy one there either. He knew of a couple of areas in Long Beach where he could buy weed or some coke, and figured he might ask one of the dealers to sell him a small handgun.

At work the next week, he approached Gerald, another meter reader, after work as they were walking to their cars in the parking lot. He knew that Gerald smoked weed because he had heard him talking about getting high and having the "munchies" with another reader in the locker room a few times. He had also smelled grass on Gerald in the locker room after work once, and had thought he had seen him toking a joint in his car before coming in to work on at least one occasion.

"Hey, Gerald, can you help me out, man?"

"Sure, dude, what's up?"

"My brother's coming in from back East. He's telling me that we've got some good weed out here and he wants to try some. I don't do it but I figured you might be able to tell me where I could get some good smoke."

"Well, I don't smoke weed either, but I heard that they sell some quality smoke up in Carmelitos. I'm told that if you drive through the north end kinda slow, some of the dealers will come up to your car. Don't flash any green, though, or you might get ripped off."

"Thanks, man. I owe you."

"Don't mention it, man. Just give me a joint or two from your lid for *my* brother."

Gerald had given him a good scoop. Carmelitos had been military housing that had been converted to low income housing. It ran from Atlantic east to Orange Avenue and from the 5100 block to the 5300 block. Each separate building contained 5 or 6 two-floor apartments and between each of these buildings were parking lots where kids, gangbangers, and drug dealers hung out at various hours of the day. At night, the dealers owned the parking lots.

That night he went up to Carmelitos and drove slowly through the area with his windows halfway down. He had been approached by three dealers before he decided that the fourth looked like one he could do business with. He bought a dime bag of weed from the guy and then told him if it was good he would be back the next night to buy "some other merchandise." When the dealer asked him what kind of merchandise he was talking about, The Skulker asked him if he could get a small handgun.

"What kind?" asked the dealer.

"I want a small pocket gun that works. I don't want any shit brands either. I want a Smith & Wesson, a Colt, a Beretta, or a Ruger. And I want a box of ammo to go with it. What will that cost me?"

"A small gun like that won't cost you much, my man. Say $200?"

"Bullshit," he said. "I'll give you $100, and I know you'll be making $50."

"Oh, man. You don't know what you talkin' 'bout," said the dealer. "Hunnert and fitty is as low as I can go."

"Just because I need the piece and I'm tired of arguing, I'll give you $125. If that ain't good enough, I'm sure one of these other businessmen can help me out," he said, nonchalantly.

"Man, you drive one hard motherfuckin' bargain, dude. How we gonna do this?"

The Skulker thought for a minute and then said, "Meet me at the McDonald's on Atlantic at 8:30 tomorrow night. Can you get it by tomorrow night?"

"Shit, man. You talkin' to a player here. Course I can," said the dealer.

"Okay, I'll be in the parking lot. You bring the gun and ammo in a McDonald's bag and come to the passenger side of my car. Once I see you ain't packing, I'll let you in and you give me the bag and after I check it out, I'll give you the money. Don't bring anybody else or I'll be outa there, understand?"

This time it was the dealer's turn to think a minute. He had an old Colt .25 auto that he had traded a couple of bags of weed for. He had thought about getting a couple of his homies together and ripping this honky off, but he could profit a full C-note for 10 minutes work before he dealt the next night and not have to cut anyone else in. "You're on, man. See you tomorrow."

The Skulker smiled to himself as he drove out of Carmelitos and southbound on Orange. He put the weed under his floormat and decided to give the whole lid to Gerald the next day for being so helpful.

CHAPTER TWENTY-TWO

*You accomplish more with a smile, a handshake, and a gun
than you do with just a smile and a handshake*
—Al Capone

October 1980. The next night, The Skulker went to the McDonald's on Atlantic. He got there an hour early, parked his car, got out, and walked into the hamburger stand. He waited in line, got some food, and sat down to eat it at a table from which he could see his car. When he was done eating, he went outside with his McDonald's bag and walked around the neighborhood west of Atlantic. It was a residential neighborhood that had small pre-World War II houses. After walking a block and a half, he found what he was looking for: a rock in a flowerbed that weighed about two pounds. He put it in the bag. He had been able to scope out the neighborhood that day when he had switched his meter reading area with Gerald, who had been exceedingly thankful for the lid of high grade weed he had given to him.

The Skulker didn't know if the dope dealer was going to try to rip him off, but he thought that he shouldn't go into the deal without some kind of weapon. He also wanted to observe his car at a distance to see if the dealer brought anybody else with him. At around 8:20 p.m., he saw the dealer go into the McDonald's and make a purchase. After devouring the hamburger in seconds, the dealer walked into the restroom and came out with his McDonald's bag in one hand, stuffing French fries in his mouth with the other. The dealer started scanning the parking lot and The Skulker thought that he was safe. He walked across the street as the dealer was coming out of the door of the fast food Mecca. As the dealer approached The Skulker's car he realized no one was in it and slowed his pace.

The Skulker walked up next to his car and motioned for the dealer to approach. The dealer increased his step. The Skulker kept his hand on his McDonald's bag but rested it on the roof of his car. The dealer walked up the driver's side door where The Skulker was standing and asked him, "You got the cash?"

"You mean you won't take a check or a credit card?" The Skulker smiled.

The dealer smiled back and said, "No, man. This is strictly a cash an' carry bidness. I got the gat and the ammo here in the bag." The dealer held out the bag for The Skulker to take.

He took the bag and opened it. He saw a small black handgun with the word "COLT" and a standing horse molded into the hard plastic grip. Except for the grey metal showing through the black on some spots you might expect a gun to wear, it looked like it was in good shape. From his research, he knew that the magazine held six bullets and that would mean that he would have seven shots if he kept one in the chamber. He also knew that this gun had a thumb safety and a grip safety and that meant that there was less of a chance of an accidental discharge. After the gun was loaded, the thumb safety could be pushed up and the gun could be placed in a pocket and carried safely until needed. And the bulge this small a gun would make in a pocket was negligible.

He also noticed with some interest that there were two small magazines in the bag and also a small box of 50 Winchester .25 caliber high velocity center fire cartridges. This was really good because these were the bullets he would have bought if he had wanted to go to a legitimate sporting goods store to buy ammo, which he didn't. He figured that the fewer people who could connect him to a firearm the better.

He reached with his left hand into his left front pocket and pulled out the roll of bills he had wrapped with a rubber band. He handed the money to the dealer and then took the bag with the rock in it and threw it at the trash can about 15 feet from his car. It hit with so loud a thud that it was apparent there was something more than a partially eaten hamburger in the sack. When the dealer saw and heard the bag hitting the trash can his eyes widened and he looked at The Skulker. Then a smile spread on his face with the realization that had he tried to rip this dude off, he might have got hit upside of his own head. The words, "Ain't this a motherfucker!" escaped involuntarily from his lips.

The Skulker returned the smile and said, "It coulda' been." He then got into his car and drove off, leaving the dealer standing there shaking his head and stuffing the wad of money into his pocket.

CHAPTER TWENTY-THREE

The end of life is not to be happy.
The end of life is not
to achieve pleasure and avoid pain.
The end of life is to do the will of God,
come what may
—Martin Luther King, Jr.

July 1981. When my partner Ted Norris and I had been working together for around a year, his wife Jeanne became pregnant with their first child.

She was due four days before my birthday on July 11th. I kept telling Ted that firstborn kids were always late and his kid was going to be born on my birthday. Ted told me that if the kid wasn't born by the 9th of July, he was going to make Jeanne do jumping jacks until she had the kid. He said no kid of his would be born on my birthday, and he wasn't taking any chances. In the meantime, Jeannie had gotten a job at St. Mary's Hospital in Long

Beach. Because they were both now working in Long Beach, the Norrises sold their house in Orange County, sold their horses, and bought a house in east Long Beach near her parents, Bill and Joan Wilcox. Jeannie's father was an administrator at Long Beach Memorial Hospital and she had kind of followed in his footsteps.

Jeanne's younger brother, Tommy, had been killed in a plane crash when he was 17. The tragedy had been devastating for all of the remaining Wilcoxes. With Jeannie's pregnancy there was some discussion regarding what to name the baby if it was a girl, but it had been decided that if the child was a boy he would be named Thomas Wilcox Norris. As Jeannie's due date of July 7th came and passed, I amped up my predictions that Ted's firstborn would have my birthday. On the 11th, my Mom and Dad took my wife Julianne and me out to brunch. When we returned home, my mother-in-law, who was babysitting, told us that Ted had just called and said that Jeannie's water had just broken and he was taking her to Memorial Hospital.

Julianne and I hopped back into our car and drove directly to the hospital. We parked and ran into the maternity waiting room, where we saw Ted's parents, retired Captain Warren Norris and Mattie. They tried to introduce us to Jeannie's parents, Bill and Joan Wilcox. I had already met the Wilcoxes, but nodded and introduced them to Julianne. We had been standing around talking and laughing nervously for nearly 45 minutes when Ted came out of the delivery room and told us all that Jeannie had just given birth to a nine pound, 21-inch bouncing baby boy named Thomas Wilcox Norris. Julianne and I started congratulating Ted and his parents. Then we turned to the Wilcoxes, who were embracing, and heard Bill, tears flowing, telling Joan, "Looks like we have our Tommy back, honey." Joan's face was also wet with tears as she hugged her husband.

At that time, I was a big, burly cop. I had been on the job for the better part of a decade. I had seen things that most people wouldn't want to see. Gut wrenching things like fatal accidents involving small children, horrible child abuse cases, murders, rape/torture victims, and other untold horrors. Through all of those things, I had been able to maintain a professional demeanor. Those might be discussed with other cops in drinking sessions after work at the "South Bay Club" or Lancers, but while at the sites of these events, I was in control. I have to admit that, knowing their history, when I saw and heard the Wilcoxes in that waiting room, I had to choke back tears. And I wasn't the only one. Captain Norris, Mattie, and Julianne were also teary-eyed.

It was the most poignant scene in my police career.

A few weeks later, my own toddler son became seriously ill. He had a cold and one night he woke up coughing and couldn't stop. We took him to the emergency room. The doctor told us that Mark had pneumonia and that it was a serious case. Mark was admitted and the poor little guy was hooked up to different medical things that he neither liked nor understood.

He wound up staying in the hospital for three days, and the first two days were touch and go. I took two days off for what the city called "Sick in Family" leave. Julianne's mother watched our daughter Margie for us and we spent the time in the hospital. Ted came to the hospital on the third day. There was a special bond between Mark and Ted. I think that Ted saw a lot of himself in Mark. Mark was a lot like Ted in that neither of them could sit still for very long. They both were like a drop of water in a hot frying pan, always moving around.

When Ted came to the hospital, he saw Julianne in the hallway, returning from the cafeteria with two cups of coffee. I was in the room holding my son. I was exhausted but relieved, since the pulmonary specialist and our doctor had just told us that Mark had turned the corner and was getting better and could probably go home the next day. We had brought a cassette player in so that Mark could listen to his favorite Sesame Street tapes.

I had grown tired after three days of Big Bird, Bert and Ernie, and the Cookie Monster so I had brought in a three cassette set of Frank Sinatra that I had been given for my birthday. When Mark fell asleep in my arms, I reached over and put on the second of the three cassettes. I hadn't even listened to the tapes all the way through and I had started the tape where I had last stopped it, which was the third song on the second side. The last song on that tape somehow really hit home with me and I had run it back so I could listen to it again when Ted and Julianne came back into the room.

The name of the song was "*That's What God Looks Like to Me.*" I'd never been all that religious, even though I had gone to twelve years of Catholic school. After starting college, I'd done what a lot of kids that age had done and stopped going to church. But after having two kids, I thought the good example would be to start going back to Mass, and Julianne, who had been a dirty, stinking heathen, or a Methodist, I forgot which, agreed to go with me. I really hadn't prayed since grammar school until Mark got sick, but you can bet I did then. Anyway, this song really hit home, and I kept backing up the tape and playing it.

I was in a kind of daze when I realized that Ted and Julianne had been standing there watching me for at least a couple of those replays of the song. When the fog lifted, I saw my wife and my partner. Ted and I were both a little embarrassed. Julianne was misty eyed. "That's one heck of a song," Ted said, ever the master of understatement.

I don't know what it was; the exhaustion, the emotional strain from my boy's illness, or the sudden memory of twelve years of Catholic indoctrination, but I found God in that hospital room, with my sick son in my arms and that song playing on the cassette player. And with that transformation came my newfound respect and dedication to the Truth.

CHAPTER TWENTY-FOUR

It's not the shit we face that defines us, it's how we deal with it
—Ahmed Mostafa

December 1981. On occasion, our plan to have our beat saturated was disrupted by normal police work. For instance, one night, a major bar fight in Belmont Shore or Marina Pacifica would require all of the Beat 9 units to respond. But, generally, we were able to have anywhere from three to five units between 2330 and 0200 hours(11:30 p.m. and 2 a.m.) out looking for and stopping any males who were in the beat.

Naturally, after a few weeks, there were fewer subjects to stop, but there was always one or two we could talk to. Most of them were legitimate. Guys coming home from work or a date or a bar, but they were stopped anyway and their information was recorded on field interrogation cards. When our supervisor, Sergeant David, found out what we were doing, he told us that he had been coming up with his own plan to try to catch our rapist, but was duly impressed with ours and wound up writing us a commendation.

About six weeks into it, our plan began to disintegrate through no fault of our own. My partner got into a shooting. I was right next to him and to this day I don't know why I didn't fire my own weapon. Here's what happened.

One of the other supervisors in East Long Beach was Sergeant Jeff Jones. All of our sergeants in our area at that time were good guys and were as interested as we were in catching bad guys. One evening, round 1730 hours (5:30 p.m.), there was a burglary in one of the high-dollar homes in Naples, which is an area of Long Beach surrounded by canals and boat docks. The description of the suspect who was seen fleeing was that of a male, Black, 5'8" to 5'10", 160 to 180 pounds wearing a grey hooded sweatshirt, Levi's, and red tennis shoes. The one officer who had actually seen the suspect fleeing had put out the description and the direction of travel, and a perimeter was set up.

We had a K-9 unit available and the dog attempted to get a track from a scent taken from one of the objects the suspect had dropped at the burglarized house. The dog followed the scent to one of the boat docks and it was assumed that the suspect had swum across the small channel to the peninsula or stole a boat at the dock. After about two hours, Sergeant Jones released those of us on the perimeter since it looked like the suspect had gotten away and there were a lot of calls for service waiting.

Around 1030 hours (8:30 p.m.), Sergeant Jones was traveling on 4th Street when he saw a Black male matching the general description of the earlier burglary suspect sitting on the bus bench at 4th and Temple. The clothing was slightly different in that this subject didn't have on a hooded sweatshirt, but he did have on a white T-shirt and blue jeans. Even more interesting was that he was wearing red tennis shoes. This was three hours after the burglar was last seen and about three or four miles away, but a good cop knows that suspects who are being chased will discard articles of clothing to alter their look. In addition, it was a somewhat chilly 59 degrees out and someone without a jacket waiting for a bus would raise a police officer's curiosity.

Sergeant Jones called for a unit to file a "shake" card on this guy so that the burglary detectives could either identify or eliminate him as a suspect through fingerprints, shoe prints, or other forensics. Ted and I volunteered, and while Sergeant Jones was eatching the subject we pulled up to the bus stop on the north side of 4th Street just west of Temple. The guy was sitting on the bench with his hands in full view on his knees so we approached him in a friendly manner. Had his hands been in his pockets or hidden from view we might have asked to see his hands prior to leaving our police cars.

This guy did not appear nervous or antagonistic, but asked us what we wanted. I told him that he matched the description of an earlier burglary suspect and I asked him where he was coming from. He told us that he had been at his girlfriend's apartment on 5th Street at Temple. He gave us her name, Tonia Reedy, and told us he had been there since around 4:30 p.m. His girlfriend and her mother had cooked him dinner and all three had sat and eatched TV until about 20 minutes before we stopped him. He told us he had to work the next morning so he had left to get the bus home. We filled out an FI on him. He told us his name was Alvin McCrea Williams, DOB of 7/11/58, and he gave us his address. He had no ID to verify what he told us.

In the meantime, Sergeant Jones was in contact with Communications and was trying to get in touch with the officer who had actually seen the burglary suspect. That officer, J. D. Tillman, a hardworking, well-respected old timer, was out of service eating his dinner and could not be raised on his radio, so a unit had been sent to get him so he could come by and see if he recognized our suspect as his burglar. Our subject told us that his girlfriend and her mother were still at her apartment if we wanted to check his story but he didn't want to miss his bus. Ted told him that if his story checked out we would take him home. So far, his story had checked the superficial truth test in that he was on the right street to catch a bus toward the address he had given as his home address. But, again, he didn't have any ID or anything with his name on it, plus his excuse for not having a jacket was flimsy. Further proof was required in our minds before we could let him go. We ran him for warrants and close to a hundred near misses came up for Alvin Williams and similar combinations, but none of them appeared to be our Alvin.

He didn't know the exact address of his girlfriend's apartment, but offered to take us there since it was only a block away. Before we put him in the backseat of our police car, I patted him down for weapons and found no obvious ones in places easily accessible— pockets, waistband, ankles, or underarms. We drove the one block to the multi-unit apartment building on the southeast corner of 5th and Temple.

He wanted to go with me to his girlfriend's apartment, claiming not to know the apartment number or for certain the location, that he got "turned around in that complex." Most experienced cops know that you don't talk to a suspect and a witness at the same time if you want to get the truth. I figured that I could find her from the name and the description he had given me.

After looking for a few minutes, I found the right apartment. It was in the mother's name and not the girlfriend's or I would have found it sooner. I knocked on the door and the girlfriend answered. Tonia Reedy was 5'10" and an attractive Black woman of around 20. I asked her if she knew a man named Alvin Williams and she told me that she did not. I described Alvin to her and she said that sounded like a friend of hers who had just left about half an hour ago. I asked her who her friend was and she said, "Willie McCrea." Her mother than came into view and asked me to step into the apartment, which I did.

Once inside, Tonia's mother stated that she did not like Willie and wasn't surprised that the police were here asking about him. Tonia piped in and said that he had arrived unexpected at their apartment door around 7 p.m. Willie had lived next door to them in an apartment on the 2100 block of Pacific until about two months prior. Tonia and her mother were just finishing up dinner and asked if Willie wanted to eat. He did so they made him a plate. Willie's only explanation for the visit was that he was in the neighborhood and wanted to see their new place as he was also considering a move. Neither Tonia nor her mother had been especially close to Willie when they lived next door to him and were surprised to see him. Willie hadn't been particularly talkative, but after eating and watching TV for an hour he said he had to go and left. "He didn't even thank us for dinner," Tonia's mother interjected.

Tonia told me she believed Willie had moved from his former apartment on Pacific, but gave me his old address anyway. Both she and her mother agreed that Willie had not used their phone to call anyone and that he seemed somewhat preoccupied and restless. I asked if they thought he looked nervous and they both nodded. I asked if they knew if Willie had a criminal record and Tonia's mother told me she'd heard he had been arrested for shoplifting at Sears. I thanked them, left their apartment, and walked back to our car and the waiting Willie.

Like an idiot, I had assumed our car had automatic door locks in the backseats. At that time some of the newer black & whites did. Apparently Ted thought the same thing. I got into the front passenger seat and turned sideways to talk to Willie. "How come you gave us a fake name, Willie?"

Willie looked surprised and then nodded and said, "No, man, my real name is Alvin Williams, but I use the name 'Willie' sometimes cuz I owe some money."

"Well then, Willie, how come you told us you had been at Tonia's apartment since 4 p.m. and she said that you didn't get there until 7 p.m.?" I inquired politely.

Suddenly, the back passenger-side door opened and Willie took off westbound across Temple. For a micro-second, Ted and I looked at each other and then I flew out of my already open door (I hadn't closed it when I sat down). As I was running across Temple I saw Willie run between two apartment buildings just north of where 5th Street would have been if it had continued west from Temple, which it didn't. There was a six-foot gate blocking his way and I thought I would gain on him, but Willie vaulted over it like an Olympic track star. When I got to the gate, I pushed it and it flew open—it wasn't locked.

I saw Willie as he left the building's property and lost sight of him as he cut southbound in the alley. As I reached the alley, I slowed and looked around the corner to the south, in case Willie had found a two-by-four and was waiting to get my attention with it. As I entered the alley, I caught a glimpse of Willie as he continued westbound between two more apartment buildings across the alley.

I decided to parallel Willie instead of following his direct escape route. My thinking was that if he decided to "jump" me from a dark area, I wouldn't be where he expected me to be. As I ran through the apartment buildings just north of where Willie had run, I saw our police car idling in the middle of the street with the driver's door open. This street was Ohio and I quickly realized that Ted had driven around the corner just as Willie had run into the street, and Ted had left our car to pick up the foot pursuit of our burglar. I ran to the black & white, got into the driver's seat, and drove southbound to 4th Street, west on 4th, then north on Molino.

As I turned onto Molino, I didn't see anybody run into the street so I slowed and rolled down my window. I heard Ted yell so I stopped the car and got out. There was a house with a long driveway from where I heard Ted. At first I couldn't understand what he was saying but then I realized that he was telling me he was in the backyard. I ran up the driveway with my gun in my right hand and my flashlight in my left. Ted came into view as I pushed the partially opened gate the rest of the way. Ted was breathing hard and I asked him if he was all right. He said he was okay and that he thought the suspect was in the bushes next to the house, but he couldn't see because he had lost his flashlight when he tried to jump the fence into the backyard.

The house was U-shaped and there was a small patio in the middle of the U. The bedrooms were apparently in the arm of the U that was closest to the alley. I shined my flashlight into the bushes underneath the bedroom windows. In my peripheral vision, I saw the inhabitants of the house, a young adult male and his wife and two small children looking out the bedroom window at us. The man pointed across the patio to some unkempt oleander bushes and stated, "It sounded like he ran into those bushes."

Ted and I took the two steps to that side of the patio and I shined my flashlight into the oleander bushes. With illumination, we saw the feet with the red tennis shoes, the legs, and the bottom of Willie's torso. Both Ted and I had our guns out and pointed at the prone body in the flower bed. Ted yelled out, "Don't move."

Almost simultaneously, Willie jumped straight up and Ted's .45 burped rudely next to me. To this day I don't know why I didn't fire my gun. I knew that I had four and a half pounds pressure on a pistol that required five pounds of trigger pull, but somehow I was able to restrain myself. Immediately after the shot assaulted my eardrums, I saw Willie fall back to the ground. He immediately started to groan. Keeping my flashlight on Willie, I holstered my gun and dropped into the flowerbed while reaching for my handcuffs. I handcuffed Willie and while Ted was getting on the radio to advise that we'd been in an officer involved shooting, call for the paramedics, a supervisor, and homicide, I pulled Willie out of the flowerbed and on to the cement patio. As I pulled him out, I expected to see blood streaks. There was no blood. We couldn't have been more than three or four feet from the suspect. Add to that the fact that Willie was still moaning and groaning and I was sure that Willie had been shot. I bent down next to him and asked, "Have you been shot, Willie?"

"Yeah," was his mournful response.

"Where?"

"In my tummy."

I rolled him on his right side and saw nothing. "You haven't been shot, you moron," I told him.

"Other side," Willie said.

I rolled him over on his left side and there were no injuries on that side either. "You're not shot!" I told him emphatically.

After Sergeant Jones and the Homicide dicks got there, we figured out what had happened. When Willie had jumped and my partner had shot, Ted's bullet had struck the ground immediately under Willie. When the bullet hit the dirt a large amount of it was blasted up, striking Willie's stomach. Being dirt and not a bullet it didn't have enough force to penetrate Willie's skin. But Willie felt like he had been shot. Willie believed he had been shot. One of the units that responded to assist us (Restrom and Russo) volunteered to take Willie to jail after the paramedics confirmed that Willie had not been shot.

Later that night, while we were filing our reports in Homicide, Russo came in and stated, "I want to personally thank you guys. We volunteered to take your prisoner to jail, thinking that we could book him real fast and go to our pop stop and order dinner before we checked back into service and asked to go nine-twelve. We thought we could get a nice peaceful code 7 that way. Unfortunately, your suspect really thought he'd been shot. He was so convinced that he'd been gut shot that he shit his pants. After smelling him all the way to the station, all during the booking process, and in the elevator up to the jail, when we were done we didn't feel like eating. Thanks a lot!"

Russo also told us something we really didn't want to hear. J. D. Tillman had come out to the scene after the shooting, but Russo and Restrom had already left to go to the Booking Desk. J. D. was able to get a good look at Willie in Booking but was unable to make a positive ID. J. D. told Russo that he could only be about 50 percent sure and couldn't be positive. Ted and I were a little upset with J. D. for that, but we didn't want him to lie. As J. D. had told us when he was teaching in the academy, "Don't compromise your honesty to put some dirt bag in jail. If he's that big a crook, you'll always have another opportunity."

Russo was able to mitigate his bad news by telling us that Willie had two felony warrants under his true name, one for possession of a controlled substance for sale and one for... guess what? Burglary. Bingo. Russo also advised us that Willie had a modest arrest record of two felonies and three misdemeanors. That didn't necessarily mean that he had committed the burglary on Naples, but it meant that his prints were on file and if he had burglarized that house he could possibly be "made on prints." On a more personal, psychological note, it meant that Ted hadn't been shooting at some poor innocent numskull citizen who had stupidly run from us in a panic.

CHAPTER TWENTY-FIVE

The criminal does not expect his prey to fight back.
May he never choose you, but, if he does, surprise him
—Jeff Cooper

December 1981. The Skulker was getting antsy. It had been two months since he'd had his last adventure, and that hadn't gone exactly as planned. True, he had escaped unharmed but he'd had to curtail his adventures. This self-imposed abstinence was causing a pressure to build in him. It wasn't so much a sexual pressure. He could cure that easily enough, the same way he had since adolescence. But he didn't get the same feeling of being fulfilled, of being in command of his universe, as when he enforced his will upon some overbearing female who needed to be taught a lesson.

Meanwhile, he had gone back to the Phoenix area to visit his obnoxious mother for Thanksgiving. He was as sweet to her as he had always been, but he had told her flat out that he would not move back to Arizona with her. He had a good job and she needed the care at the nursing home. When she begged him to take her with him, he looked around the day room and nobody was within hearing distance. He had wanted to tell her that he didn't want her anywhere near him; that his father, who had left when he was only five years old, had the right idea. But he just said, "No, that's not possible."

He remembered the arguments. He recalled how his mother had berated his father. She had yelled about how he was a poor provider, how he was a bad father and a poor husband and a "piece of shit as a lover." He remembered his usually mild-mannered father just couldn't take it anymore and, after coming home drunk for the first and only time, told his mother that she was a "ball-busting, controlling, suffocating bitch," and he wasn't going to take it anymore. This was, of course, after she had again berated his father for his laziness, his cowardliness, his stupidity, and for having saddled her with their "insufferable brat." He remembered his father finally slapping his mother. Rather than being upset, she seemed to get excited by the slap. She had begged for more. She questioned his father's manhood until he slapped her again. He had been afraid and hid in the kitchen. For the first time his father was standing up to his mother and she seemed to *enjoy* it. He was confused.

Things then became quiet, and when he peeked from his hiding place he saw that his father was on top of his mother and they were kissing. He ran out the back door and walked around the neighborhood for an hour. When he came back, his mother and father acted as if nothing had happened. His mother appeared to be a little more kind to both him and his father for a couple of days after that, but it didn't last. A week later, his mother was her usual obnoxious critical self to his father.

A few weeks after that, his father went to work and simply never came home. With his father gone, and his mother having no one else to heap her scorn on, she began to criticize everything he did. He had taken it for years until one day he stood up to his mother and told her to "shut the fuck up or I'll kill you when you're asleep." This would not have been hard to do. After his father left, his mother had made him sleep with her until he was 13. His father had come back into the picture for six months at that time and found out about his mother and him sleeping in the same bed.

His father had a new family now and was still making child support payments, but he told The Skulker that he couldn't move in with this new family because his new wife wouldn't allow it. His father had lived in Las Vegas for eight years, and asked him if he had gotten any of the birthday or Christmas gifts his father had sent him. He had not.

His father told him that he had tried to call after the separation, every week at first, but The Skulker's mother wouldn't let him talk. His father had come back to Phoenix for six months to set up a new branch office for his new company and when he found out that his son was still sleeping in the same bed with his ex-wife he had blown a gasket. His father had told his mother that this was "unhealthy." He had bought The Skulker a new bed, brought it over to the house, and put it together in the second bedroom. He gave The Skulker his work phone number and told him to call him whenever he needed anything.

His father then told his mother that if he heard about his ex-wife sleeping with her son again, he was going to call Children's Service and/or the police. He had hidden his father's work phone number, but before he could memorize it, his mother apparently found it and destroyed it.

Just as The Skulker was feeling pride in his father for standing up to his mother, his father went back to his new family and he was left alone again with his mother. His mother, of course, told him how his father had abandoned them both again. His attempts to contact his father never proved effective. He had the name of the company, but every attempt to get his father's home number proved futile. Apparently, his father had left orders that his home phone number was not to be given out to anyone, and he was sure that his father did this to keep his mother from harassing his new family.

As much as he hated his mother, he also was attracted to her. She was a good-looking woman and although he hated what she did to him when they had slept together, he also found it exciting. He hated to think what a psychiatrist would say. He knew the Oedipus story and could see its relevance to his life.

Yet he had come back to see his mother this last Thanksgiving. He couldn't cut the old apron strings completely. He had also thought that he might be able to have an "adventure" in Phoenix.

This last thought had turned into a reality. He was staying in a cheap motel near his old neighborhood. On Friday morning, the day after Thanksgiving, he went to a McDonald's for an Egg McMuffin and a cup of coffee. While he was sitting there in the patio section, a woman in her early 30s drove up in a newer red Ford Bronco. She had two kids in the car, a boy, five-ish, and a girl about seven. She waited in the car for a few minutes and an older Chevy pickup drove up and parked next to her. A man roughly the same age as the woman got out of the truck and walked up to the driver's side of the Bronco. The woman began to yell at him through her open window. The man apologized for being one minute late and leaned in and asked the children to get into his truck. Once the kids were in his pickup, she really let him have it. She told him how irresponsible he was and it was just like him to be late.

She told him that her new boyfriend was a professional football player and had to be at the airport in less than an hour to fly to San Francisco to meet his team. She was going to be home and could have kept the kids. She also said that he was to have the kids back to her new home by five o'clock on Sunday or she would take him back to court. She then rattled off her new address and her ex had to go get a pencil and a piece of paper from his truck. She repeated it three times and The Skulker made a mental note.

The Skulker went to his rental car, pulled out the road map of Phoenix that the rental company had conveniently given him, and found the street. He went back to his motel room, put on his jogging suit, and drove to the woman's neighborhood. He spotted the red Bronco parked in the driveway of a modest tract home and then drove past it a couple of blocks and parked. He ran down her street slowly, taking in all of the hiding places and locations of streetlights and porch lights and other lights used for outside nighttime illumination. He looked for where he thought the shadows would fall when these lights were on at night. He also looked for possible escape routes that wouldn't be readily noticeable at night. At the end of her block, he made a left turn to see if there was an alley or a vacant lot or unoccupied house nearby. He was in luck. There was a major addition going on in the house immediately behind hers and it looked as if the owners were away for the Thanksgiving weekend. There were three newspapers in various locations on or near their driveway.

After he made his first pass, he jogged by again and noticed that there was a window on the side of her house that was open. The screen on that window would pose no problem to him if the woman left it open at night. He decided he had seen enough in the daylight and would come back at 7:30 p.m. to see how things looked at night. He ran back to his rental and drove back to his motel room to take a nap before going to see his mother.

After visiting his mother, he went to eat at a local café. He was already in his jogging suit and he was excited about the possibility of having another adventure, so he ate lightly. When he was finished, he paid the bill and left the waiter a large tip, at least by his standards. He drove to the woman's neighborhood and parked at the same place he had in the morning.

By the time he did his stretches, it was almost 7 p.m. It was dark and the streetlights were on. He took a leisurely jog in a figure eight circuit that took him by the woman's house five times. He was able to look at the lights and shadows from both directions. He could tell where he could stand unseen and which escape routes were the safest. It was too early in the evening to do anything. He knew that he had to wait until most of the people were home from the bars. It would have been easier if this had been a work night, but he figured that the night after Thanksgiving would find most righteous citizens worn out by the festivities from the day before. After jogging and making more mental notes, he made his way back to his rental car then back to his motel to catch some shut eye until his new adventure could begin.

At 1:45 a.m., he awoke from a restful sleep. He put on his jogging suit and shoes and went to his car. His jogging jacket had been modified to hold his lockpicks; all he needed were two, a torsion bar and a pick. They would slip into the lining on the bottom and even if he were stopped and frisked by the cops they probably wouldn't even feel them. He had brought his good knife but not his Colt .25 auto, which he had disassembled and placed in two different pieces of luggage that he had checked in with the skycap.

After his last adventure in Long Beach, he thought he might need to bring the gun. But then he thought that the cops weren't looking for him in Phoenix, so it would just get in the way. The knife on the other hand was wicked-looking and would scare the woman into submission if she saw it before he pulled her nightgown up… if she wore a nightgown. And if she felt the blade on her neck, she would definitely become compliant.

He drove to the woman's neighborhood and parked at a different location. He backed his car almost right up next to the car behind him. Arizona only requires back license plates and he felt that if someone thought the rental looked suspicious they would have a hard time reading it without moving the car parked behind it. He jogged toward the woman's house and was able to see that her Bronco was still in the driveway.

He looked around, trying to look like he was not looking around, and then while still at a jog, kind of sidestepped into the shadow of a tree in the parkway. He stopped and stood still for a few minutes, catching his breath, and looked for the next place he could get to in order to remain unseen.

He looked around and saw that there was no one else out on the street and no cars within sight. Her saw that the shadows between the woman's house and the one to the east were only about 25 feet from where he stood. Even though there were streetlights, they were spread wide enough that he wouldn't be illuminated when moving between the shadows.

In his mind, he went over some of his provisional measures. He had taken the dome light bulb out of the socket so that the light wouldn't go on when he got in or out of the rental car. He had a spare set of clothes in the backseat of his car under a blanket to change his look if someone got a description of him. He had his knife. He mentally went over escape routes he had seen earlier in the evening. He was ready to go. He moved quickly and smoothly to the shadows between the houses. He saw the window that he had seen earlier and although it was closed more than it was in the morning, he could tell that it wasn't locked because it was still a quarter of an inch from being completely shut.

After he shut his eyes for a few moments so they could adjust to the darkness, he went to the window. He was able to noiselessly pull the screen off and silently slide the window open wide enough to pull himself through. He sat a short time on the floor of the living room and listened. He heard nothing, which was good. He crawled on the plush carpeting. Since he had not had a chance to reconnoiter or see a floor plan and was not familiar with this neighborhood, he thought it would be safer to crawl along the floor, thus avoiding tripping over or into some piece of furniture or wall he didn't know was there.

He entered what looked like a hallway to him. He knew instinctively that the woman's bedroom was this direction. He took his time, relishing in this part of his hunt. He stopped crawling for a minute and took the knife out of his sock. He stood up and there was just the hint of a creak in the floorboards. Silently, he listened, and heard nothing.

The woman was a light sleeper. Something wasn't right and she knew it. As she lay awake on her bed she wondered what had awakened her, but she knew whatever it was it was out of the ordinary and she waited to hear it or sense it again. A minute later, she did.

Just the very slightest of a noise in the hallway. She had never taken a self-defense class, but she had grown up with three brothers, all within five years of her age. She had hit and kicked and wrestled with them until she was sixteen when she decided (or rather her mother and father had decided for her) that it was time for her to start acting like a lady. Het brothers had been told to leave her alone and let her "be a lady." She still played softball and volleyball for her high school, but her relationships with her brothers became more restrained or formal. They still teased her, however, and she teased them back. Timmy, her younger brother, had told her that she was the strongest girl he had ever seen. Her older brothers agreed.

The woman was only slightly afraid. Then she realized that she was strong and with a plan there was no reason she couldn't "win" in most situations. She also remembered what her oldest brother John had said, "Ninety-nine percent of all fights are won by the guy who throws the first punch." She knew her ex-husband had the kids so she didn't have to worry about anyone but herself. She was going to go for it.

She slid out of bed and went to the door to the hallway. Whoever or whatever was out there was just a few feet away. She knew what she had to do. She jumped suddenly into the hallway and saw a shadowy figure three feet from her bedroom door. She punched with her left hand at the center of the figure and connected. She saw him raise his right arm and she took her right foot and kicked out as hard and as high as she could, striking the man's forearm. She knew now that she was fighting a man. She heard something hit and bounce off the wall and land on the carpet in the living room. She then moved forward, punching with her right and left fists. She drew back her right foot again and kicked as hard as she could. She connected with the man's left side. The intruder fell backwards and then was up on his feet, across the living room, and out the window.

The woman was surprised and stopped for a moment in stunned silence. She ran to the phone in her bedroom and called the police. She didn't see which way the man had run and she really couldn't give much of a description since it had been dark in her house. She told the dispatcher that she thought that she had injured the intruder. She said that after she kicked him the last time she knew that he was hurt because even though he was moving very quickly he seemed to be listing to the left.

The dispatcher told her that she would stay on the line until the police arrived. The dispatcher asked her if she was injured at all and she replied that she was not. She added that she actually felt pretty good. The adrenaline was still coursing through her body and she felt like she had just drunk a whole pot of coffee.

She felt exhilarated. She had met a challenge and had overcome it. When the officers arrived, they knocked on the door. She jumped a little, even though she knew that the officers were at her front door because the dispatcher had told her they were walking up her porch. It had only been a couple of minutes since she had called.

At first, the officers acted as if this were a routine call, but when she showed them the window and they found the screen laying on the ground they seemed to get a little excited. When she told them that it could not have been more than four or five minutes since the suspect had left, one of the cops got on his radio and asked for other units to assist in setting up a perimeter. Then he asked for one of the other officers who took fingerprints to assist. He started asking her questions and writing her response on a report on his clipboard.

***

The Skulker knew he had a broken rib or two. Every time he took a breath, fire shot through his left side. He was so pissed off. The bitch had kicked him as hard as he had ever been struck. He was able to stop momentarily in the shadows about half a block away and gather his thoughts. He knew he had to follow his prearranged escape route. He had it all mapped out.

A police cruiser came flying by when he was halfway to his rental car. He stood completely still in the shadow of a tree until the cop car passed. He didn't have to look. He knew it was going to the woman's house. He counted to ten after it passed, then made his way to the next shadow. He knew he didn't have much time now. He hurried, but carefully. When he reached the rental car he quickly opened the back door and climbed in. He laid down on the backseat and pulled the blanket over himself. He knew he would be there for a long time. If he heard anyone coming near the car he would slip to the floorboards no matter how much it hurt.

Just two minutes after he jumped into the backseat, he heard the distant roar of police cars coming into the area at high speed. He tried to relax but his ribs were killing him. He took inventory and knew that in addition to his ribs he would be bruised on his right arm and his entire chest. He had been lucky the whore hadn't hit him in the face. Clothes would cover his visible injuries and no one would suspect he had been hurt.

After about three hours, he looked out the window and could not see any cop cars. He heard a car start and ducked down again. After the car passed, he looked up and saw that it was just a regular passenger car. After a half an hour, he heard another car go by. He gingerly climbed over the front seat. He started his car, turned on his lights, and drove slowly out of the neighborhood and back to his motel.

At the motel, he went to his room, found the ice bucket, and went to the ice machine down the hall. He went back to his room and made an ice pack from a plastic garment cover in the closet, laid down on the bed, and put the ice on his cracked ribs. It was only marginally more comfortable than his rental car's backseat. He lay there fuming. Someone was going to have to pay for the pain this bitch had caused him. And although he didn't feel it right at the moment, The Skulker knew that his urge would be even more intense when his pain was gone.

CHAPTER TWENTY-SIX

Plans are things that change
—Fujio Cho

February 1982. During an administrative hiatus from my regular partner and my regular beat, I was working with Russo, mostly in North Long Beach, but we worked downtown and in East Long Beach, too. One night, we heard the call go out of a rape that had just occurred in the 1400 block of Orizaba. Had we been working my beat that probably would have been our call. We rolled toward that address and I slowed the car down about three blocks away. I turned out our lights and pulled to an empty place by a curb near a corner and started watching. I looked down Orizaba and Greg looked down 17th Street for any movement and anyone crossing either street. Greg picked up the mic and gave communications our location. Three other units had quickly placed themselves in a perimeter and gave their locations. We didn't see anyone. Neither did the other units, except one that saw an elderly lady in a bathrobe chasing her cat down the street. They helped her with the cat and asked her to please stay in her apartment for the rest of the night.

We waited for a suspect description, and after a few minutes the graveyard unit that had gotten the call put out the general description that could have fit half the men in Long Beach. A little later the unit put out some additional information that made me think it was the same rapist Ted and I were looking for. First, there was no sign of a forced entry and, second, the rapist had bitten both of the victim's nipples, one completely off. Not only that, but the victim had been beaten much more severely than in the prior rapes.

Greg and I both thought that the suspect must have been locked up in jail and that time in the slammer must have pissed him off, so now he was taking it out on his victims. After the perimeter was broken down we went and talked to one of the officers, Jay Kawalski, who was handling the report. He told us that the suspect had beaten the victim with his fists, concentrating on her rib cage. The paramedics told him that she had at least four broken ribs. The suspect had used such words as bitch, whore, and cunt when referring to the victim and also said things like "that'll teach you to kick me" and "how do you like it" while striking the victim. It was only after he had beaten her that he was able to make penetration.

Because the suspect was getting more violent with his rapes, we felt that there would be further rapes with increasing violence. From one of my criminology classes I had taken at Long Beach State, that seemed to be the pattern in these cases.

Kawalski also showed us some evidence he had found near the front door of the victim's apartment. I knew from my days in Juvenile that it was a torsion bar, a little piece of spring steel, L-shaped, that was used in picking locks. That made sense. We had wondered how this creep was getting into locked apartments and houses without the usual forced entry. Now we knew. I made a mental note to let Homicide know about the lockpick.

Two days later, Sergeant Ron Cussion thanked me for the information I had left in the form of a memo regarding the lockpick. He said that eventually it might turn out to be very useful, if they could connect the rape on Orizaba to the double murder. "When we find the guy, if he has any lockpicking or locksmithing experience, this will help convict the asshole."

As I was heading to my car, I saw the Watch 3 Booking Sergeant, Carl Robbins, walking toward the tunnel entrance. I knew Carl had a master's degree in psychology and was working on his doctorate. I told him about the rapist/murderer and that I thought his crimes were getting more violent. I told him that the rapist had laid low for three or four months after the double murder and had just started up again. Carl told me that not only would his rapes become more violent, they would probably increase in frequency. I thanked Sergeant Robbins for his help and told the other cops what Robbins had said. We were going to have to go back to our plan. Sergeant David was off work that night but we thought that we could again resume our surveillance by the end of the week.

CHAPTER TWENTY-SEVEN

Nothing seems to tempt fate more than mentioning
the possibility of something bad happening
—Donald G. Firesmith

March 1982. After three weeks of working with Greg, Ted and I were back together in our regular beat. Our first night started out real crappy. There was an injury accident with the injured being a little girl.

When we arrived at the scene we saw that a 1979 Ford Galaxy had been side blasted by a brand new 1982 Lincoln Continental. The injury was to a three-year-old girl who had been standing up on the front seat in the Continental.

The paramedics arrived shortly after we did and started working on the little girl whose head had broken the windshield. Thankfully, she did not go through the windshield, Even though she had a few minor cuts on her head, it could have been a lot worse. She was crying softly. It bothers you that you can't do more for a child in pain. You also can't help but think of your own kids. You try to act like you hope some other cop or paramedic would act if it was your child in a similar situation. Basically, we just had enough time to comfort the child by telling her that everything was going to be all right, and help console the driver, who was the girl's grandmother, before the paramedics arrived and started first aid. Both of us wanted to throttle the grandmother for not having the little girl in the back seat with at least a lap belt on, but her "verbal throttling" would come later at the hospital.

Despite the grandmother being partially responsible for the injury to the little girl, the other driver, who had turned left in front of her, was the cause of the accident. The California Vehicle Code states that when making a left turn a driver must wait until it is safe. If an accident occurs when a driver makes a left turn, it obviously wasn't safe. I was up to take the report and after getting the information from the other driver, I cited him for the left turn violation. I also talked to a couple of witnesses, and after Ted took the measurements of the point of impact and the length of the skid marks, we went to St. Mary's Emergency Room to get grandma's statement and driver's license information.

The little girl was not injured too seriously but the doctor told us they were keeping her for observation. I was not going to cite grandma since at that time there was no vehicle code section for not having a child in a car seat or other restraint. Plus, I figured she was feeling guilty enough as it was. I was going to warn her that she could be arrested for child endangerment if she allowed a child to stand up in the front seat of a moving car again. As I started to inform her about these dangers, her husband, who had joined her at the hospital, got in my face and told me I didn't know what I was talking about. He was so obstinate, strident, and obnoxious that I had Ted go back to my car and get a citation book and cited his wife for child endangerment anyway. That was usually a misdemeanor, but I could have arrested her for a felony since the child was injured. I knew, however, that the District Attorney would never file it.

When Grandpa accused me of just ticketing his wife because he was arguing with me, I simply smiled. I found out later that the City Prosecutor read my report and said, "Yeah, I'll file this." Grandma was found guilty at a trial at which I testified, and fined $500 (about $425 more than the guy who turned left in front of her). Grandpa glared at me the whole time I was on the stand. But I digress.

The second call that night was a peeping Tom. I stopped our car in the middle of the alley where the perpetrator was reported to be, and Ted and I both jumped out and told the guy we saw to stop, which he did. The guy looked like a solid citizen in a brown tweed suit and clean-cut look. Ted asked for his ID and the man produced a wallet with a Nevada driver's license, which Ted had him take out of his wallet.

I went to the apartment building about twenty yards up the alley where the suspect was supposed to have committed his peeping. As I was walking to the back security gate, a heavyset middle-age woman was unlocking it. When she saw me she asked if we had caught the guy who was peeping at her daughter.

I explained to her that we had the suspect stopped but we did not catch him looking in any windows. She said she had come out to the alley to dump her trash and she saw him looking in her sixteen-year-old daughter's bedroom window. She said she knew her daughter was changing clothes to go to her choir practice at church. She told me that she ran back into the house and called 911 and then went to her daughter's room to get her daughter out of there. The woman then informed me that when she saw the man looking in the window, he also saw her and stood there for a moment or two before turning to walk away.

Ted and I had only been half a block away when the call went out and so the suspect hadn't even made it to the end of the alley before we arrived. I explained to her that since we didn't actually see the suspect committing the crime, which is a misdemeanor, and she did, she would have to make a private person's (citizen's) arrest. She just looked at me and said, "What do I have to do?"

I explained that she would have to identify the man. Before I could explain anything else she looked around me toward where Ted and the suspect were standing, and said, "That's the man that was looking at my daughter while she was undressing." I then told her that she would have to tell him he was under arrest for being a "Peeping Tom." She started walking toward him and when he looked at her, she said, "I'm placing you under arrest for trying to peep at my naked daughter, you motherfucker."

That was close enough for me, but the suspect shook his head and said, "You're crazy." Ted told him to place his hands behind his back, which he did. When Ted had one handcuff hooked on the suspect's right wrist, the guy said, "This is bullshit," and the fight was on. While I had been talking to the victim's mother, a few of the local gang bangers from the East Side Longos had gathered to watch. They were just curious, but we also knew that they weren't going to help us at all.

Anyway, the suspect wasn't very big at five foot seven inches, but he was pretty stocky at one hundred and sixty pounds. And it turned out he was exceedingly strong. Ted put his arm around his neck and started to apply the carotid restraint, commonly called the "choke out." Now, Ted at six feet and two hundred pounds had size and weight on the suspect. When he threw the suspect over his hip, Ted also had leverage. I didn't think that the suspect would stay conscious for another ten seconds, so what happened mystified and scared me. The guy was able to reach up with both hands, one manacled, and grab Ted's arm and pull it from around his neck.

At that point, I grabbed my nightstick from its holster and started striking the guy as hard as I could on his shins. I knew I was hitting him with a lot of force, but it seemed to have little or no effect. Ted, in the meantime, again applied the carotid hold and again the suspect pulled Ted's arm away. This went on long enough that my arms were getting tired swinging my baton like a baseball bat. The Longos found this to be most entertaining. The lady who had placed the suspect under arrest just stood there looking disgusted. I knew how she felt. Finally the guy said, "What do you want me to do?"

"Put your hands behind your back and quit resisting," Ted yelled. To our amazement he did just as he was told. Ted leaned him up against our patrol car, finished handcuffing him, and patted him down for weapons. As we were placing him in the back of our car I saw that the legs of his tweed pants were cut in several places where the nightstick had struck his shins.

The Chief had started a new policy that required officers who had used force to notify their supervisor. So I had communications notify Sergeant David, the East Sergeant. We thought this was a stupid policy and Sergeant David didn't think much of it either. He asked us what had happened, and he talked to the lady who made the arrest and some of the Longos who had witnessed it. He said he guessed he had to file a short memo. Then he sent us on our way to Booking.

At the Booking Desk, the suspect lifted up his pants legs and showed us his shins. There were numerous bumps and a couple of places where I had broken the skin. I told him that none of those would have happened if he would not have resisted. He acknowledged that what he had done was stupid. He said he didn't think I had broken any bones but we were both surprised that I hadn't. After we booked the prisoner and took him in the elevator up to the jail, we went down to the first floor and filed our arrest and crime reports. The stenos in Reporting told us that we were the busiest cops in the city. That day, I believe we were.

When we left the station we were thinking of going code seven, but before we had gone a block, we saw an obvious drunk driver going the wrong way on Broadway with his lights out. He had an early seventies Buick Wildcat, a midsize car at that time. When I activated the red lights and sirens, the drunken sot, who was coming at us, pulled his car as far to the right as he could and momentarily stopped. I was in the middle of making a U-turn when this jerk hit the gas, burned rubber, and started to flee at a high rate of speed, going the wrong way on a one-way street. The worst part was he was heading toward a freeway off-ramp and it looked like he was going to be using it as an on-ramp.

By this time in my career, I had been in shootings. I had seen people die. I had rolled on armed robberies in progress. I had chased felony suspects on foot, up dark alleys by myself, not knowing if they were armed. I don't remember being afraid during any of those incidents until after they were over and I had time to think what might have happened. But I can say without a doubt that as I hit the accelerator to catch up with this slob, I was as scared as I have ever been in my life.

My thoughts were these: If I chased this guy up the off-ramp and the wrong way on the Long Beach Freeway it might cause him to go faster and there was more possibility of the suspect, an innocent driver or passengers, or us being killed. If I didn't chase him he would probably kill himself or somebody else because he didn't have his lights on. In less than a heartbeat I decided to chase the drunk because at least with my flashing red and blue lights it would give some warning to other drivers that there was danger heading toward them.

Ted grabbed the mic and put out the pursuit. He advised them we had a wrong way driver heading up the off-ramp at Broadway.

We weren't lucky enough for this jerk to turn before reaching the off-ramp that he seemed drawn to like a sailor to a bar. The drunken slob continued westbound on Broadway, past Magnolia and Daisy, and onto the off-ramp. We were fortunate in that there was only one car coming off the freeway when the dumbass started up it.

The off-ramp for the southbound Long Beach Freeway is two lanes and curves to eastbound on Broadway. We saw the Buick heading up the ramp at about seventy miles per hour. I had my foot on the brake ready to stand on it when I saw the headlights of another car coming at the Buick. I was hoping that my flashing lights and sirens would attract the other driver's attention and somehow convey the message to stop immediately, pull to the right, and by the grace of God, stay out of this maniac's way, but by this time I had enough experience to know that flashing lights and sirens are rarely seen or heard until the last second.

Somehow the Buick went to its left and around the headlights. I whispered a prayer of thanks to a good and merciful God when I saw that the drunk had oversteered his Buick after passing the oncoming car, had glanced off the left siderail of the off-ramp, and then went across both lanes and spun out. Some dust and debris blossomed up in the air. I had stomped on the brake, but when the car coming toward us stopped, I shot by it and pulled up to where the Buick had stalled across one lane and about a quarter of the lane on the left. There was enough room to get by the Buick so our lights could be seen by other cars heading toward Broadway. Ted and I both jumped out at the same time, but I got to the driver's door first. The drunk driver, who was not wearing a seatbelt, had banged his noggin on the doorpost of the Buick and was a little stunned as well as being half in the bag.

I don't mind telling you that my adrenaline was pumping and when I grabbed the cause of my anxiety, pulled him out of the car, and slapped him across the face, I was thinking of throwing him headfirst off the ramp and onto the concrete below. I might have too, if Ted hadn't reached around me and grabbed the guy by the throat in a C-clamp and told him to put his hands behind his back. Ted took control of our prisoner and after handcuffing him, put him in the back seat of our car. He radioed for other units to assist us and to divert traffic further up the freeway.

Neither Ted nor I were gentle with this death defying drunk. But when you've just had an experience where you think you are going to die and adrenaline is coursing through your system like creek water in a flash flood, it is near impossible to stop one's emotion from overriding one's reasoning. I'm not justifying it, I'm merely presenting it as an extenuating circumstance that should be considered when judging a cop's actions. Most seasoned officers know this and will step in to stop an adrenaline-infused officer from going over the line.

Other units arrived. One of them volunteered to take the collision report and got our statements. Also, the citizen who had almost had a head-on collision on the off-ramp with our idiot had stopped at the side of the road on Broadway and gave a statement to the reporting officer. After I had set out a flare pattern, there were enough units that we could leave and take our prisoner to the station. Before we got into our car, Ted and I looked at each other over the top of the car. Shaking my head, I held up my hand so Ted could see it shaking. "That scared the living shit out of me," I said quietly.

"You? You were at least driving. You had some control. All I could do was hold on and wait to die," Ted responded, his usual booming voice now muted.

We drove the short distance to the station, booked our prisoner, who blew a .23 blood alcohol (.08 being considered drunk for driving purposes at that time), and filed our reports. Again the stenos commented on Ted and me being the hardest working cops in the city.

As Ted and I started driving back to our beat. I told him how much fun I'd had the last night working with Greg Russo and that the first night back with him we'd had nothing but crappy calls all night long. After almost getting killed chasing a drunk driver the wrong way up a freeway off-ramp. I told him that the way things were going tonight, we would probably get a week old, bloated, reeking dead body call after we ate.

Ted, unusually agreeable, said that everything I had said was true. However, he argued that he was not a jinx. He told me that all of these things happened because I was the jinx. I patiently explained to Ted that since I had come up with the jinx theory, it was impolite of him to steal it and turn it back on me. The gentlemanly thing to do, I advised him, was to come up with his own theory to explain our "bad moon rising" night.

Ted thought for a minute and then said, "You always say that bad things happen to assholes. You're an asshole. These bad things are happening because you're an asshole. They're only happening to me because I'm with an asshole."

I thought for a moment and then turned to Ted and said, "That's a good theory, except that bad things didn't happen to me when I worked with Russo." Ted said, "I can explain that. Russo is an asshole too. It's like 'two negatives make a positive,' you know what I mean? Two assholes make like a decent individual, much like myself, so bad things won't happen to them when they work together." I wasn't buying it, but Ted had just driven into the parking lot at Omega Burger on Anaheim and Ohio, and it was time to eat and not to discuss philosophy. Once we ordered our food and sat down, the discussion switched to food. Omega Burger made a pastrami burrito that is the size of a meatloaf and was so mouth-wateringly good, I would almost commit a felony to get one.

After we ate, I cleared us on the radio. We weren't back in service for two minutes when I started feeling like a clairvoyant. The dispatcher's voice cackled our call sign and dispatched us to a dead body call at an apartment. One of the tenants had found the owner/manager dead in bed. She hadn't seen her in two days and thought she smelled gas. The owner was a friend and had given her a key to the apartment to feed the owner's cat when she occasionally went away. The tenant went in and found her friend in her bed, dead.

Ted was saying that I had put a curse on him since he was up for the report and was babbling about how working with an asshole caused all this bad stuff to happen to a nice guy like himself. But Ted's luck was changing. One of the graveyard units was training a recruit and the training officer volunteered to handle the call because he wanted his recruit to handle the dead body report and possibly see a dead body for the first time. Also, the rookie could experience the odoriferous delights that often accompany the deceased.

We were just about to swing through our beat for the last time that night before heading back to the station when the graveyard unit advised us that we should meet them at the location of the dead body and then asked for a supervisor and homicide.

When we arrived at the apartment, the training officer, Jim Powers, advised us that they had found no sign of forced entry or a struggle. When they went into the bedroom, they found the woman in bed, covers pulled up to her head. There appeared to be some bloody and foamy vomit next to her head, which was tilted to the left. The bedding was somewhat disheveled but not anything that might cause them to think that there had been any foul play. Because the woman was only 39 years old and had been in otherwise good health, Powers had the rookie call for the coroner.

When the coroner pulled back the blanket and sheet, they realized that the woman had been murdered. Her nightgown was pulled up to just under her neck. Both nipples had been bitten off and there were bite marks on the breasts and thighs. The coroner said that it looked like she had been smothered, probably with a pillow, and then her body was posed. Powers knew of our plan to catch the murdering rapist and asked if this looked like his work. I told him that I was sure it was our guy. I also told him what Sergeant Carl Robbins, the unofficial department psychologist told me, that the rapist's crimes would become more frequent and more violent. I asked Powers to advise the other graveyard units that this murdering sonofabitch was active and killing again. If we didn't get him soon, it was only going to get worse from here.

CHAPTER TWENTY-EIGHT

To punish someone for your own mistakes or for the consequences of your own actions, to harm another by shifting blame that is rightly yours; this is a wretched and cowardly sin
—Richelle E. Goodrich

March 1982. The Skulker had to get even for his humiliation in Phoenix. He knew who the most likely women were. He knew who lived in his area and who were the most vulnerable. Still, he did his homework once he returned from what he thought of as his Thanksgiving fiasco. Then he remembered one woman in particular. Marilyn McNulty was the most obnoxious woman he had come across in a long time. She apparently owned her own business and worked out of her apartment in East Long Beach. She had something to do with managing apartments and other properties. He thought she owned the apartment building that she lived in—at least, she collected the rents from the other tenants.

The building was in the 700 block of Termino, a quiet neighborhood that had both private homes and apartments. While reading his meters over the past year, he had heard the McNulty woman reaming people out over the phone and screeching at tenants for rent. Her major offense was chewing him out for stepping in the flowerbeds when reading the meters. How the hell was he supposed to read the meter from eight feet away? He had meekly acquiesced and mumbled an obsequious apology. He was pissed for hours at his cowardly response to her unreasonable complaint and he knew then that he was going to make her pay for that. And now she would pay for what happened in Phoenix, too.

Due to the different types of houses and apartments in the neighborhood, his recon was fairly easy. There were lots of trees and two-story apartments to shade large areas. In addition, the door to the McNulty woman's apartment was in a major shadow from a large elm tree 20 feet from the door. The streetlight was right in front of the tree, effectively putting the whole front landing in the dark.

In addition, the building was only around thirty yards from 7th Street, which was a major thoroughfare in Long Beach. He could park his car on 7th and it would attract no attention coming or going at practically any hour. Another positive for this area was there were three construction jobs going on in that block. It had become profitable for speculators to buy single family dwellings on large lots, bulldoze the house, and put up a six-, eight-, or ten-unit apartment building. That meant safe hiding places if he were caught in a perimeter, although he had heard about the city getting more K-9 units so that they would have dogs on all shifts every day.

He had gone back three nights in a row and thought that this was the best location he had ever seen. He knew that McNulty went to bed at 11 p.m., and apparently watched late night TV until 12:30 a.m., when her bedroom light went off.

On the night of this adventure, he had all of his equipment on his person. His lockpicks were in his hidden pocket, his gun was in its hidden holster, and the gloves were stuffed in the front of his jogging pants. He was in his running outfit and had his running shoes on.

He parked his car on Termino in front of one of the construction sites so that he could see when McNulty's bedroom light went off. He didn't park on 7th because cops always traveled the main streets and would probably notice a man in a parked car and might stop and ask questions or make a note of the license number. He would move his car to 7th Street after the bedroom light went off.

At 12:35 a.m., her light went off. He started his car, drove around the block, and found a spot to park. He exited his car and started jogging. He jogged around the block a few times and checked his watch. It was now 1:05 a.m. He jogged into the shadow of the tree in front of her apartment door and stood until his breath was even. He got out his lockpicks by feel and slowly and carefully walked to the front door. He found the keyhole and, using a pick and torsion bar, picked the lock in about ten seconds. He heard a clink on the porch and knew that he had dropped his torsion bar. He took a moment to feel around for it, but couldn't find it. He wasn't worried. Like all good lock pickers, he had extra picks.

He opened the door quietly, stepped in, and softly closed it behind him. He stood and waited. He listened and looked. He saw a nightlight coming from the bathroom. The bedroom door was closed. The door to what he knew to be her office was open. When he thought he had waited a sufficient amount of time, he walked slowly toward the bedroom.

Once in the bedroom, he saw that Marilyn McNulty was fully asleep. He wasted no time. He pulled his gun, walked over to the bed, and put one hand on her mouth. When her eyes jumped open in shock and fear, he started to get excited. He leaned down and whispered in her ear, "Don't move or scream, bitch, or I'll blow your head off." He put the gun barrel next to her head to punctuate his remarks. He knew that she knew it was a gun. He put it back in his jogging suit jacket pocket.

Then he pulled back the covers. She was wearing a long flannel nightgown. He let his hand fall from her mouth, ready to put it back if she started to scream, but he didn't think that she would after feeling the gun at her temple. In the dim light, he could still see the fear and became more excited. He reached down and pulled the nightgown up over her head. She was naked underneath. He started fumbling with his pants and they got twisted. His excitement was starting to diminish. By the time he finally had his pants lowered, he had lost it, but he knew what would increase it again.

He bent down and bit her breast. That was when she started screaming. The nightgown did little to lessen the sound. He grabbed the pillow and placed it over her head. Then he raped her and bit her in a frenzy, while the victim thrashed under him with all her might trying futilely to get a wisp of air. He punished her for the humiliation he'd felt in Phoenix. He brutalized her for the humiliation she'd caused him when he stepped into her flowerbeds. He held the pillow tight to her face for a long time after she had stopped struggling.

When he was done, he took his time and posed her in her bed. He pulled the nightgown down from her face but left it up around her neck. Then he pulled the covers back up under her chin so it looked like she was asleep. In a last rattle, she foamed a pinkish substance from her mouth.

He took his time cleaning up. He didn't take off his latex gloves until he left the apartment. He was able to lock the door from the inside without having to get his picks out and re-lock it from the outside. He jogged around the block to his car on 7th and, after a furtive glance around, jumped in, retrieved his keys from under the mat, started it, and drove home.

This killing was deliberate. The kid and the aunt were unintentional, but not this bitch. She deserved it. And The Skulker felt good about it. He also felt sated. It had been a long time, too long, but his itch had finally been scratched.

CHAPTER TWENTY-NINE

It is what you don't expect... that most needs looking for
—Neal Stephenson

March 1982. It had been three weeks since the rapist/murder had killed Marilyn McNulty. Ted and I and the other cops who worked beat nine were not allowed to reinstitute our plan to catch the thug. The Chief and his administrators decided (correctly, I thought) that the public needed to know that there was a serial rapist/murderer in Long Beach. We, the cops who worked the beat where most of the rapes occurred, thought that we should be given the opportunity to catch the guy, but the administrators played to the media and started a "task force." There were advantages and disadvantages to this. The advantages were that the cops assigned to the task force would only be working on this until they got him or the rapes and murders stopped. They wouldn't have to answer calls for service or be distracted by other things like traffic tickets or reports. They would meet with the homicide and sex crimes detectives on an almost daily basis and the flow of information would be better.

The downside was that those guys didn't know our beats as well as we did and we had to get them up to speed on this dirt bag. They didn't have all of the information we already had and they weren't asking for it. In law enforcement, sometimes, there is a proprietary feeling about information an individual cop obtains. When it came to catching bad guys, though, neither Ted nor I felt that it was as important that *we* catch the crook as someone—anyone—caught the sonofabitch. We went to the first task force meeting. The commander in charge didn't want us to go, but the homicide sergeant told him what we had done so far and we gave all the information we had to the six-man task force (which also included a sergeant, a lieutenant, and a commander so the media could be told that there were nine people working on it, even though the lieutenant and the commander really had only been put in charge as overseers and had other responsibilities).

By this time, the rapist was being called "The Phantom" by the task force, more for the purpose of the media than anything else. And, of course, the media made him look like he was superhuman. He entered buildings without a key and escaped without leaving a trace. No one had seen or heard him except his earlier victims, and their descriptions did not really match each other. The pressure was on the Chief and the department to get this guy. We wanted to get him, too, but the main thing to us was to get him off the streets and stop his spree. I was hoping that The Phantom Task Force would snuff him out and call the Press-Telegram in to take front page photos of his dead and bloody body.

That kind of publicity has a chilling effect on crime.

The night my dilemma started, the task force briefed us on what they had done. There had not been any rapes for three weeks. The task force had been given an office and they brought in a pin map of the locations of the rapes they and the Sex Crimes detectives thought The Phantom had committed. There were 10 of them including the homicides, more than Ted and I had thought. And even though all 10 of them were in East Long Beach, only six were in our beat. Two of the others were in Signal Hill, one in North Long Beach and one right on the other side of the line between our beat and Area One.

The Sex Crimes detectives had informed the task force, who in turn told us that all of the rapes and/or rape-murders were believed to have occurred on Tuesday through Friday mornings between 0030 hours and 0330 hours with most occurring between 0200 and 0300. Since none had occurred on the weekends, the task force was looking into the possibility that the rapist was doing time on the weekends. Outside of that they thanked those of us who had gathered information and Field Interrogation cards on possible suspects and said they were checking it all out.

The task force worked 10-hour shifts from 1800 to 0400 hours (6 p.m. to 4 a.m.), Monday through Thursday, but their shifts and days off were subject to change if The Skulker changed his modus operandi. We went to work as usual after the Squad Meeting. It was Wednesday, January 12, 1983. It's a date I'll never forget. It was actually early the next morning that I was shot and thought I was dying, but since my shift started on the 12th, that's the date that comes to my mind every time I think of it. It was then that my dilemma started, when I executed the murderous, cutthroat, cowardly piece of shit who had killed at least three people, including a small child, and raped ten or more others. He deserved to die and I'm certainly not sorry I did what I did, but it did cause me some moral consternation. Not the killing but the cover up, which I really had no direct part in. But as a result of what happened later that night, I remember everything that happened before like it occurred yesterday.

Our shift started out as usual. Our first call was a non-injury accident report at 7th Street and Newport. I was up for the report and in about an hour we had all of the drivers' information, measurements, and the finished report, and had given one driver a ticket for making an unsafe left turn and had given both drivers the forms with the report number for their insurance.

I had finished the report before it was my turn to drive so when we were dispatched to the 2400 block of East 3rd Street for a residential burglary report I was still up for that one, too. That really wasn't a problem, since we could call in all the information to a device in records and they would type out the report later. All I had to do was fill out the face sheet of the crime report, write a few notes where the narrative would usually go, list what was taken in the burglary, get a report number, and call it in.

The victim was a man and his wife in their early forties. The man had gone to work at 6:30 a.m., and his wife had left the house at 7:15. The man returned from work at 5:30 p.m. and found that his front door was unlocked and the color TV, stereo, and a clock radio were gone. I checked the front door and it looked like the burglar had used channel locks on the knob to open the door. I wrote my notes, asked to use the phone, and called in the report. I kept the face sheet of the report just in case the machine didn't record all of my report or it "got lost" somewhere in the system. We switched drivers when we got back to the car.

We then handled a family dispute where a daughter wanted her mother arrested for battery because the mother had slapped her across the face when the daughter called her a "fucking bitch." The mother had told her that she couldn't drive the car the next Friday night. After talking to the mother and the daughter it was apparent that the daughter had the attitude problem. We advised the mother, in front of the daughter, that she had every right to slap her daughter when she showed such blatant disrespect. We also advised her that the daughter could be taken into custody as an incorrigible if the daughter persisted in not obeying her mother. (This was really kind of a bluff since incorrigibles at that time required a lot more on the part of the daughter than just a slap.) We then advised them of the downside of being placed "in the system." When we left it didn't look like daughter would call the police on Mama again, at least when mother was in the right.

By the time we got back to our car, it was 20:45 (8:45 p.m.). Before clearing ourselves for another call, we stopped at the hamburger stand at Ximeno and Anaheim and bought some takeout food to take to our buddy Maxwell's apartment on the peninsula in Belmont Shore so we could Watch *Hill Street Blues*. When we pulled in front of his apartment, we cleared the family dispute and asked for nine-twelve. We were cleared for code 7, went into "The Maxwell's House Café," and had a leisurely dinner while watching the show. At a commercial break about 40 minutes after we checked out on the radio, we checked back in. There were no calls holding at that time so we finished watching the rest of *Hill Street Blues*, then went to our car and drove back toward Redondo Avenue.

At Ocean and Granada, we saw two men arguing and gesturing at each other. We could tell that it was going to turn physical. We put ourselves there on the radio and jumped out of our car as one of the men took a roundhouse swing at the other, missing him by a mile. I grabbed the guy throwing the swing and placed him in the carotid restraint hold, but I didn't apply any pressure. Ted placed himself between me and the swinger and the other guy who had started to come at us. When he saw Ted, the guy stopped and thanked Ted.

In the meantime, the man I had in the hold started to struggle. He also started yelling in a shrieking voice, calling the other guy a faggot and a whore and a cocksucker. Since this was a gay neighborhood near a gay bar, it was apparent to Ted and me, even before we stopped, that this was a lover's quarrel, probably a drunken one. At the sound of these insults, the recipient instantly angered, did a quick sidestep around Ted, and threw a punch at the screeching voice which was obnoxiously close to my ear. He would have landed the punch, too, if Ted hadn't reacted swiftly to the sidestep and shoved him just as his punch was about to land. Rather than striking the screamer in the mouth, the fist glanced off my shoulder.

At that point we knew both combatants were going to jail. There was an unwritten rule at that time that if you "put hands" on a citizen, you had to take him to jail even if you had to "humbug" him (an arrest where the suspect has not violated a criminal statute, but is arrested for "contempt of cop" by being overly obnoxious). The fact that we saw these two would-be boxers arguing in public, using words that would likely cause a fight, and that they indeed swung at each other made these individuals arrestable for disturbance of the peace and fighting in public. The fact that they were in close proximity to a bar made it at least an even bet that one or both of them was legally intoxicated. And the reality that one of them had actually struck me with a closed fist made that fella a candidate for battery on a police officer.

The easiest arrest report to do was "drunk in public," which basically meant just filling out the booking sheet and writing a short paragraph that the suspect was so intoxicated that he was unable to care for himself or others. A fighting in public report was a little more elaborate and would take us an hour or so from the start of the booking process to driving out of the Booking Tunnel with everything done. A battery on a police officer report would take even longer, and we really never considered booking the guy who hit me for that charge, the main reason being that I wasn't injured. Second, the suspect didn't intend to hit me, he was trying to hit the guy I had in a carotid hold. In a report for battery on a police officer, you have to show the intent to hit him. I'd been in uniform so there was no problem showing that the suspect knew I was a police officer, but all four of us knew that he was trying to hit his screeching boyfriend and would have succeeded if Ted hadn't misdirected his punch. We could have written it up in such a way that the suspect looked guilty of battery on a police officer, but for one thing it wasn't true. For another, the report would have taken us the rest of our shift and the DA or City Prosecutor most likely wouldn't have filed it anyway. Another huge reason for not reporting it as a battery on a police officer was that if too many of those reports are filed, it would make it less likely that a really good case with an injured officer could be successfully prosecuted.

At any rate, we decided that even though both of these combatants were borderline drunk, it would be worth the extra time to file our reports as fighting in public. After we booked both of them, we got cups of coffee, found a steno, and filed our reports. I did mention in the body of the report that the number two suspect struck me while attempting to hit his co-combatant, thinking a judge might see that and increase his fine. We filed our paperwork, drank our coffee, bantered with the stenos, went to the booking tunnel, got into our black & white, and drove out of the tunnel and directly to my dilemma. At the time it was 0:23 (12:23 a.m.)

CHAPTER THIRTY

Misdirection. What the eyes see
and the ears hear, the mind believes
—John Travolta

March 1982. After he killed the McNulty whore, The Skulker started to cut out the newspaper articles, mostly from the Long Beach Press Telegram, which had the most coverage, but also the small article in the LA Times. It seemed to praise his abilities to enter and leave homes without a trace. The papers attributed "several" rapes in East Long Beach to him and were looking at perhaps a dozen more that he may have committed. One of the articles had an interview with an expert who had stated that the rapes/murders would now become more violent and more frequent. The expert stated that he hated women, had probably been abused by his mother, and that the killings were probably the result of some recent traumatic experience. Apparently, he felt guilty and wanted subconsciously to get caught, according to the expert.

The cops in the articles had advised women to make sure their doors and windows were locked, and if they had alarms to be sure to use them. One even made the suggestion that they put something in front of their doors that would fall over and make noise when the door was opened. All of the information in the newspapers and the one TV news report he saw got him thinking.

The so-called expert had pretty much hit the nail on the head in part of his analysis of The Skulker, but he wasn't even close on the rest. He did hate women, his mother had abused him, and he knew he was getting the urge more often. But he didn't feel guilty at all. Those bitches deserved it. And he sure as hell didn't want to get caught. He knew he wasn't going to leave any more victims alive. He wanted to punish them and could think of no greater sentence than death.

He knew from his readings that the cops had a task force looking just for him now, but he wasn't worried. He had his gun, which was highly concealable, he had his skills with opening locked doors, and now, thanks to the papers, he knew what to expect when he opened one of those doors. He would look for alarm signs and avoid them if he could, or defeat them. He knew how to beat most alarms from his days as a locksmith. Also, he had talked to the cops before and knew how to act meek to put them at ease. Besides, if he had to resort to using his gun on a cop it was no big deal. He actually considered the formation of a task force a good challenge.

He thought that he would be able to show the cops for the stupid routine bureaucrats that they were. They were no match for him. What would the newspapers and TV say after his next adventure? Among the many books and articles he'd read on tactics and covert operations, he had read one by a former Navy Seal that had talked about a method that the author had likened to a "misdirection" play in football. This was perfect for The Skulker's next outing. He was going to misdirect the cops.

CHAPTER THIRTY-ONE

The evil that men do lives after them;
the good is oft interred with their bones
—Shakespeare, Julius Caesar

March 1982. As we left the station, before we could even check back into service, the dispatcher for East Long Beach put out a notice of a man in dark clothing seen walking into bushes next to an apartment building in the two hundred block of St. Joseph. Although this was generally south and east of most of the rapist/murderer's activities, it wasn't that far away. The task force had said that with all of the publicity The Phantom was getting, he might change the area in which he was operating as well as some of his M.O.

All of the task force units advised the dispatcher that they were in route to that location, and all other units were advised to stay out of the area. Ted and I thought that this was bullshit. We thought the Belmont Shore unit would be the closest and could get to St. Joseph Street a lot faster than any of the task force units. We were proved wrong when one of the task force units checked in 10-97 (at the scene) within two minutes.

Although the regular patrol units in East Long Beach were told to stay out of the area, we knew that most of them would be in and around Belmont Shore in case this dirtbag slipped through the task force's perimeter.

We thought that this might be the rapist murderer, but it was a long shot. It was probably just a peeping Tom. Belmont Shore, with a large population of attractive young professional women and coeds, drew more than its fair share of peepers. At any rate, there were plenty of units already in the area, and as much as we wanted to get this asshole, we figured that the rest of our beat needed to have a police presence, so we headed up to the north end of our beat. We were stopped at the signal at Redondo and PCH when we heard what sounded like a woman scream. As Ted and I looked at each other, almost immediately we heard another scream that sounded liked the word "help" cut short.

Ted was driving so I grabbed the microphone. Before I could speak, one of the units down on St. Joseph put out a foot pursuit of the possible rape suspect. Both Ted and I had handheld radios, so we figured we could put our location out when the foot pursuit ended. The screaming had come from one of the rear apartments south of the Executive Suite Bar at the northeast corner of PCH and Redondo. Ted drove east on PCH and south on Newport. He turned off the headlights as he made the turn onto Newport. He coasted to a stop behind the covered carport at the rear of the building. I saw the numbers painted on the beam above the garage, 1760. "1760 Redondo," I said out loud so that when the foot pursuit was over one of us could put out our location. The apartment building was a complex that consisted of 2 two-story buildings with a patio and a swimming pool in the center. We didn't know where exactly the scream had come from, but I told Ted that I would take the south side of the south building. I didn't want him to set me up like he had before by telling me that it was my turn to take the back of the building.

Ted seemed to go along with my suggestion, and when we got out of the car he headed toward the north building while I headed for the south one. The foot pursuit was still going on so we both turned our radios down. I had my flashlight in my left hand and my .45 auto in my right, listening for any sound that might indicate a struggle in one of the apartments in the building. There was a gate leading into the complex and I saw Ted go through it. I decided that I would go to the outside of the south building. There was another two-story apartment building south of 1760 Redondo and between them there was a walkway that was somewhat overgrown with weeds and ivy. About half the windows were missing their screens, and the screens were on the ground looking like they had been there for a while so I wasn't drawn to any particular window as a place where an illegal entry might have occurred. I shuffled along, trying not to make any noise when I stepped on the vegetation. I stopped and listened, and looked up at the south building at 1760.

There was a muffled sound coming from the patio area, but I couldn't be sure if it was Ted moving some of the pool lounge chairs or what. I knew Ted would have yelled if he needed help. I turned off my flashlight and stood still, trying to listen and/or see any activities. Suddenly, from the building behind me, I heard a window slide open quickly. It was a first story window around six feet above the ground and about fifteen feet closer to the rear of the building than I was. As I turned my head I saw a dark figure jump to the ground, I raised my gun and shouted "Stop! Police!"

From the shadow that had landed in a squat position, I saw a flash and felt a fire in my right side. I was wearing a bulletproof vest that was advertised to stop anything short of a rifle bullet, but I knew the bullet didn't hit my vest. It had hit under my arm above the vest or between where the front and back pieces were.

I fired twice with my .45 at the crouched shadow and sensed it falling backward. I really couldn't see because I was temporarily blinded from the muzzle flash. I heard a whimpering from the room the figure jumped from but that wasn't my focus. As my vision came back to me I saw the figure writhing on the ground and I saw a small gun at the feet of a man in dark sweats. When he saw me, he put his hands up and said, "You shot me in the knee, man. I give up. I give up."

I recall faintly hearing Ted yelling in the distance, asking if I was all right, but Ted wasn't my focus then either. As a matter of fact, I was losing my focus. I knew I was dying. It wasn't like the cliché stories of your life flashing before your eyes. Quite the contrary. What I saw was the rest of my life fading away. I saw myself pulled out of the church when escorting my daughter up the aisle in her wedding dress. I saw my wife sitting alone watching my son at his high school football game. I felt the sorrow my wife felt as the flag was removed from my casket, folded, and handed to her. I saw Ted in his own piss-poor inadequate way trying to comfort her, and I felt his sorrow too. I saw my little boy and little girl sitting next to their mother wishing she would stop crying and not fully realizing the magnitude of the loss of a father. I saw my mom and dad, my sisters, and all of my friends and cop buddies, and I knew the void they were feeling. I had felt it before at other police funerals. I saw all this and felt all of this and I was as angry as I ever had been. This miserable lowlife sonofabitch had just fired the shot that was killing me as I swayed there, and he was calling "I give up" but I couldn't do anything.

These thoughts were flashing through my head at lightning speed even as the darkness was closing in. I had come to work that night expecting only to do my job. I had no intention of committing any crime or hurting, injuring, or mortally wounding anyone except in the protection of myself or others. Now I saw my future flying away, my family and friends suffering, and their lives changed forever. And right in front of me was the agent of this evil situation. Why should he live? Even if he didn't get away, he might get lucky and spend the rest of his life in prison, while I was dead. He had a chance of not even being convicted. No, I thought. If I'm going to die, so is this sonofabitch. What could they do to me anyway? Fire me? After I died?

I knew I was dying fast. I could hardly breathe and I was losing my balance. I started stumbling toward him. I could barely keep my gun pointed at the asshole. There was a second of recognition and I knew we had talked to him when we were looking for the rapist. I staggered to three or four feet away from him. He said, "Don't shoot!" and put his left hand up in front of his face, palm out, as if to ward off the bullet. But it was too late. I had made my decision. By force of will I stayed conscious, although the blackness was closing in on my vision. I dropped to my knees so my .45 was only inches from this murderous cutthroat baby-killing ass-wipe. With all of the strength I had left, I pulled the trigger just as the blackness covered everything.

***

Meanwhile, Ted had gone into the courtyard. He had been doing the same thing I had been doing, listening for sounds of a struggle or more calls for help as he quickly and quietly moved around the pool furniture to the north building. He didn't hear anything until he heard the two shots in rapid succession, the second one much louder than the first.

From the echo and the sound bouncing off the buildings he couldn't quite tell where the shots came from, but he assumed they were from me and/or a suspect.

He yelled, "Ed, are you okay?"

Getting no response, he ran back toward the rear of the courtyard. He already had his gun drawn and his flashlight in his left hand. When he got to the back gate, he looked around the edge into the south part of the carport and didn't see anything. He called for me again but, instead of getting a response, he heard another loud report. It sounded like a .45, which he knew was my gun, but bad guys often had them too as there was a large number available as surplus from the Armed Services. Ted knew exactly where this shot had come from: the south side of the south apartment building at 1760 Redondo. He knew that was where I had gone. Ted quickly ran to the corner and peeked around, then hit the scene with his flashlight.

It took a second or two for what he saw to register in his mind. When it did, he pulled his radio from his belt and yelled into it, "Nine, nine, nine (officer needs help) and nine-nine-eight (shots fired)—officer down." He didn't immediately get a response because another officer was running the subject he had caught in the foot pursuit. Ted yelled into his radio again, "Charley Nine. Emergency clearance. Officer down. Nine-nine-nine. Nine-nine-eight. Roll paramedics to rear of 1760 Redondo."

I was lying on my back on the ground still clutching my .45. The suspect was lying on his back about three feet to the side of me. He had his hand over his face and there was a bullet hole in his hand that had passed through and struck the suspect right in the middle of his forehead. Ted could hear a severe wheezing and knew it was coming from me. But he also heard another sound that made him look up from the carnage. It was a sobbing, and it came from a window on the apartment south of 1760 Redondo.

The woman was bleeding from a scrape mark on her head, which was all Ted could see of her. She was crying uncontrollably, and he asked her if she was all right. When she shook her head he told her that the paramedics were coming.

Ted came running over to me. He knew from his Academy training that the sucking sound I was making meant that I had been shot in the lung. He started looking around for some plastic or other thing to put over the wound so I could at least keep some air in it. He took my pulse. I had one, but it was weak. While he waited for the other cops and the paramedics to arrive, Ted took my gun from my clenched hand. He also found the suspect's gun, a .25 auto. He left it where it had fallen and leaned down and told me that it was okay, I was injured but I was going to make it and the paramedics were arriving now. (Ted told me later that he thought I was almost dead and he wouldn't have been surprised to hear a death rattle come out of me.)

Ted heard help arriving and shined his flashlight at them as they were driving past so they knew where to find us. When the paramedics arrived, they cut off my shirt and vest and immediately slapped a non-porous bandage over the wound and took my vital signs. Ted said they had me out of there in less than three minutes, but it seemed like hours to him. They rushed me to the emergency room at Community Hospital, only a few blocks away.

Somehow, another paramedic unit responded either just for practice or in response from a call the first paramedic unit had made. They went into the apartment to work on the woman who turned out to be the last victim of The Skulker.

CHAPTER THIRTY-TWO

It's your reaction to adversity, not adversity itself
that determines how your life's story will develop
—Dieter F. Uchtdorf

March 1982. Ted directed the first patrol unit that arrived to interview the girl in the apartment since she looked like the only witness—until all the other windows started lighting up and opening to see what all the commotion was about. Sergeant Johnny David was the supervisor who responded to the scene and he called for Homicide, which handled all of our officer-involved shootings. Sergeant David instructed other units to guard the scene and not to let anyone in until Homicide arrived. He then took Ted to his car and had him explain the whole incident to him. He asked Ted if he needed anything or if he wanted a POA representative or anything, even though Ted hadn't fired a shot or seen anything.

Sergeant David had been on the job over 30 years and had worked Homicide for more than five years before making sergeant. He had looked over the scene and pretty much knew what had happened and in what sequence. He knew that I had executed this dirtbag after I had been shot by him. He knew that he had a possible witness and he found out soon enough that this was the suspected rapist-murderer.

Sergeant David then radioed in to check on me in the hospital. They told him they didn't think I was going to make it. He knew that if he covered this up he might get into some criminal type trouble, but he didn't care. He knew that if I was found to have executed the rapist, regardless of the justification, my wife and kids could possibly receive no pension or other survivor benefits. He knew I wasn't a crooked cop on the take and he knew me well enough to figure out that I had executed the murdering rapist only after I thought that I was mortally wounded. He knew with every fiber of his being that Justice, with a capital J, demanded that he cover up this execution. He also knew he couldn't do it by himself.

Sergeant David walked around to the front of the apartment where the eyewitness was being attended to by the paramedics. She had bite marks and bruises over her upper torso and head. The paramedics had stopped the bleeding from the bites and calmed the victim down somewhat. She was ready for transport to the hospital, but Sergeant David stopped them and asked if he could speak to her alone for a minute.

Once they were alone, he told her how sorry he was that this had occurred. He told her that rape and assault victims sometimes think that they are themselves at fault and keep replaying the crime over and over in their minds. A victim might think that if she had done this or that differently the crime would not have occurred. Sergeant David told her to resist the temptation to think that way, if at all possible. He told her that she should have a right to expect to be safe in her apartment whenever she was there and that bad people had no "right" to commit crimes.

He then asked her if she had seen what had happened outside her window. The victim, whose name was Nora, told the Sergeant that the rapist had stopped suddenly when he heard something outside her window. He had put a small gun to her head and told her that he would kill her if she made a sound. He then stood up, pulled up his sweatpants, and peeked out the window. What he saw apparently scared him because he opened the sliding window and jumped out.

Nora said she immediately got up, pulling her nightgown down as she did. She was going to close and lock the window so the rapist couldn't get back in. Just as she reached the window she heard a pop and then a loud bang. She saw the rapist fall backward, drop his gun, and grab his leg. Then she saw movement to her right and saw the policeman. He was staggering and wheezing. She saw the officer point his gun at the rapist and, as he got closer to the suspect, she heard the rapist saying something about giving up. The policeman waivered for a second or two and then pointed the gun at the rapist from only a foot away. The rapist raised his hands and the cop shot the rapist through his hand, and she thought the bullet also hit the rapist in the eye. The officer then fell to the ground and shortly after another cop came into view.

Sergeant David told Nora that she was extremely lucky. For one thing, the sergeant believed that this rapist was The Phantom who had killed at least three people and raped close to a dozen. For another, this guy was now dead and she wouldn't have to worry about him ever coming back to finish what he had started out to do. Sergeant David next told her he was going to be honest with her. The officer that had killed this miserable piece of shit was still alive although it didn't look like he was going to make it. He told her that if the officer lived and she told anyone else what she had seen, the officer could be tried for murder. He also told her that if the officer died and she told her story, his wife and kids would not get his pension because he was killed while committing a murder.

Nora told the sergeant that the officer had saved her life. She asked him what she could do to help him. This was what he had been waiting to hear. He knew that once she was committed to helping the officer who had saved her life, they could devise a story that would fit the evidence.

Sergeant David knew that it would be easier if he told the Homicide detectives what he was doing, but he also thought this was a burden that was best carried by him alone. The Homicide dicks would be skeptical, but would have to believe Nora if her statement matched or nearly matched the evidence. From his experience, Sergeant David knew that the rapist would have gunpowder burns on the hand that he had held up in his futile attempt to ward off Ed's bullet. Quickly formulating the story in his mind, Sergeant David told Nora to tell the Homicide detectives the same story exactly as she had told him up to the point where the rapist dropped the gun. Sergeant David told her that the suspect didn't drop the gun, but held on to it as the officer ran toward him. The officer then fired as he was stumbling forward.

Nora repeated the story twice and didn't vary from one rendition to another.

Sergeant David then took her over to the paramedics to be transported to Community Hospital. He told her that the Homicide Detectives would contact her at the hospital. The radio on his hip then coughed out the information that the Homicide Unit was 10 minutes away and rolling to the scene.

Sergeant David then went to where the dead suspect was being guarded by one of the graveyard officers. He told him to wait out front until Homicide arrived and then direct them to the body.

After the officer was out of sight, the sergeant went to work. The gun was about 18 inches in front of the suspect's right foot. This made Sergeant David think that the rapist was probably right-handed. He looked around. At that time, nobody was looking out their rear windows down at the scene. Most of the action was happening in the courtyards of the two apartment buildings where the cops and the paramedics were. He strolled close to the gun and nudged it with his foot closer to the right side of the body. Then, he walked around to the other side of the body and, once again looking around at the windows of the two apartment buildings and seeing no one watching, he reached with the toe of his shoe and pushed the dead rapist's right hand, which was laying across the front of his body, to his right side. It landed with a dull thud next to the gun. Sergeant David then walked to the rear of the apartments and waited for the Homicide Detectives to arrive. Justice, he thought, sometimes had to be helped to its proper conclusion.

The two Homicide Detectives on call were Phil Francois and Frank Hyatt Taylor. Sergeant David briefed them on what had occurred and salted his story with his altered facts and made some "helpful" suggestions based on his former homicide experience. He told them that I was in Community Hospital and that the eyewitness/rape victim was also there. Sergeant David ended his statement to them by telling them that Ted was standing by in the front of the apartment to give his statement and do a walkthrough if they needed one from him, but since he didn't fire any shots, Sergeant David didn't think that was going to be necessary. He also told the detectives that it looked like I was in bad shape and was unconscious when he last heard. He requested that they release Ted as soon as they got the required information so he could go to the hospital to be with me.

I didn't know any of this had happened for a month because I was in surgery, doped up, and then slipped into a coma for some inexplicable medical reason. The first person I remember seeing when I did wake up was Julianne. It seemed that the doctors and nurses had told her that I was going in and out of consciousness and that it was only a matter of hours before I "came out of it." For the first week after the shooting, Julianne had spent almost every waking hour at my bedside. The kids stayed with her parents. She later told me that, after the first time she saw me, deathly pale hooked up to oxygen and monitors, she didn't want the kids to see me. She told me later that she "knew" I was going to die and she didn't want the kids' last memory of their father to be of me hooked up to all kinds of medical devices and looking like a corpse in that hospital room. After the first week, the nurses told her to just come back during visiting hours and to stay at home and take care of the kids and they would call her when I made any progress.

When I first woke up, I tried to ask her where I was. I had no memory whatsoever of what had happened. Julianne told me that I had been shot and almost killed, but that I was a hero. In the gunfight, she said, I had killed The Phantom. She said that she heard from some of the cops who came by to visit that I was going to get the department's Medal of Valor. She held my hand and I could see the tears well up in her eyes. I tried to speak and when I did it came out as a harsh croaking whisper that was completely inaudible. After my first few attempts at words, I couldn't even manage a croak.

It was just as well because the memories started coming back to me. Oddly enough, the first thing I remembered was Ted telling me I was going to make it. After a few post-shooting hospital recollections had come back, the whole shooting experience returned. I thought of what Julianne had said about me getting the Medal of Valor and I thought that there was no way, there had to be some mistake. I started thinking that Internal Affairs would be coming to grill me as soon as I was able to talk, or maybe a DA's investigator or a couple of our own Homicide dicks. More than likely the FBI would do the investigation and a federal prosecutor would try to nail me for violating the murdering rapist's civil rights. After this initial panic, however, I realized that if anybody in authority knew what had happened I would be in the jail ward at County General Hospital. I calmed down and went to sleep with Julianne holding my hand.

When the doctors and nurses who had worked on me during and after my operation came in the next day, I couldn't express my thanks for all their help because all I could do was croak. One of the nurses told me that my vocal cords had constricted because of a month without use and an oxygen tube down my throat but it would improve and I would be able to talk again soon. Once the word got out that I was back among the living (and conscious), all kinds of cops started coming in to see me. This really buoyed my spirits, even though I couldn't tell them that. One or two of them told me not to try to speak. They had been told at the squad meetings that I wouldn't be able to for a week or more.

After my first aware day, Ted brought me a large notepad and a pen and pencil and I was able to start communicating in the slow laborious way that a weakened, shaky invalid does. There were cards and letters from all over, even two from outside the U.S. There were also two or three dozen cards from a couple of local elementary school classes that the teachers had kids make up during art class or whatever that Julianne read to me. Some of them were hilarious and I saved the best ones for the cops who came to see me. These kids' sentiments really meant a lot to me, and the way that kids think gave me a charge and I think helped speed my recovery.

I was in the hospital for three weeks after I came to, and during that time I was learning how to talk again, how to breathe again, and how to walk again. Late on the first night that I became aware of things, I was awakened by Sergeant David. The nurses were very protective of me, and I wondered how he could get in to see me after hours when none of the other cops would even have tried to get by the nurses. But Sergeant David was a big boisterous guy who knew a lot of people around town, having grown up, gone to school, and worked in Long Beach his whole life. He knew half the hospital staff and all of the doctors sitting on the board.

When Sergeant David knew I was awake he told me that he knew I couldn't talk but asked me to nod my head for "yes" and shake it back and forth for "no." Then he asked me if I understood and I nodded. Sergeant David then looked me in the eye and asked if I remembered what happened and I again nodded "yes." He didn't flinch, but continued to question me. "Did you think you were going to die?" I nodded.

"Was the suspect holding the gun when you shot him the first time?" I nodded. "Okay, don't shake or nod your head again. I'm just going to tell you what I think happened based on what I saw at the scene. Don't panic. I fixed it and you're in the clear. I think the first exchange of fire, you hit him in the knee and you took a shot to your right side. This shot clipped your lung causing it to collapse and making you believe that you were dying. The suspect's gun was on the ground and he'd fallen backward so the gun was not within reach. You think you're about to die and you thought that when you expired he could get the gun and kill your partner or the rape victim or whatever, and before you passed out you stumbled over and shot this shithead through his left hand and into his head as you were falling into unconsciousness.

"Now let me tell you what I did. I moved the gun next to his right hand so it looked like he still had the gun when you killed him. The only witness is the rape victim and she told the Homicide dicks that you stumbled toward the suspect and fired as you fell toward him and that he was trying to shoot you. That's what Homicide thinks, that's what the Chief thinks, and the evidence at the scene and the eyewitness corroborate it. Homicide will talk to you when you're able, but nobody's going to dig too deep. They'll just ask you enough questions to close out the case. That's what happened and we won't talk about this ever again, got it?"

I nodded and Sergeant David winked, turned, and walked out of the room. He looked down the hallway toward the nurses' station, then returned to my room. In a matter of fact tone, he said, "The suspect turned out to be a guy named Pete Parkinson. He worked at Edison and got the information on his victims and their houses and apartments when he was reading the meters. They found lockpicks in a hidden pocket in his sweatshirt and a special holster for his gun. In his apartment, they found articles of the rapes and murders. He came from Phoenix and the cops there think he's good for six or seven rapes there before he moved to Long Beach. What I'm saying, son, is that you did a great public service. I don't think you feel all that bad about it, but if you're feeling in the least bit guilty—don't." Sergeant David then patted my shoulder, said goodnight, and left.

Sergeant David had covered for me. I knew that he'd told me this so that I would also know that if Homicide was going to go after me (not a very likely scenario), I would know how to answer the questions, and if I didn't answer them correctly I could burn him. I knew that he'd risked his career and freedom to save my sorry ass and that gave me an even greater love and respect for the man.

While I was still croaking inaudibly, Francois and Taylor came to see me. After asking me a few questions and getting responses only a frog could understand, I started to write out my responses. Taylor stopped me and told me that if they needed anything, they would come back again when I was speaking. He also told me not to worry and started to ask me yes or no questions that really never touched on whether I had executed the rapist.

When they were done asking their questions, Francois turned to Taylor and said, "That ought to give us enough to close this case out. What do you think?"

Taylor just nodded and told me, "Good job." Francois winked and the two Homicide detectives left.

And that was it. I was never asked if I had executed the suspect who had shot me after he had dropped his gun, and I certainly wasn't going to volunteer the information. With what Sergeant David told me, it looked like I was going to skate. I didn't feel guilty. As a matter of fact I felt pretty good, like justice had been done. I'm not saying that cops should kill violent suspects they catch in the act when the suspect is willing to give up. I do believe in our legal system when it isn't overburdened with restrictions that are more geared to creating "proper form" than finding guilty people guilty and innocent people not guilty. But, in certain circumstances, there are times when justice is better served at the scene with the police officer as the judge, jury, and executioner. I thought this was one of those situations.

I suppose, when I was able, I could have gone to Homicide and told Francois and Taylor exactly what I had done, but bad things would have happened. I might have been able to sell it as within the shooting policy, not to mention state law, due to the fact I was losing consciousness and that would have possibly allowed the suspect to get away and thus put the women of Long Beach in mortal jeopardy. That would have been true, but try selling that to the anti-police press that was prevalent at the time. If the press had gotten hold of that, I would have been fried. The

Chief of Police at the time wasn't bad, but he would have had to be one hell of a ballsy guy to face the heat and stand up for me. It wouldn't have happened. The Chief serves at the pleasure of the City Manager, and the City Manager would have caved in to media pressure and given the Chief the ultimatum to fire me or face the same fate himself.

Now, those who live in the fantasy world of legal theory would say that it's wrong for a cop to act as judge, jury, and executioner because one is innocent until proven guilty. Okay. But in the real world, in an alley in the dead of night, the asshole shooting at you is guilty as sin. If he gives up and you're able, the good cop has an obligation to take the shooter into custody and let the legal process take its course. But my situation wasn't addressed in any case law I'm aware of. In my case, there was a shootout. I thought I was mortally wounded and consciousness was ebbing quickly. The suspect was not mortally wounded. He wanted to give up, but I wasn't *physically able* to take him into custody. Was I supposed to just wait until I went unconscious? He was near enough to his gun that he could have retrieved it within seconds and administered a coup de grâce to me and then faked like he was dead and killed my partner when he came to investigate the shots he heard.

At that moment in time, my thought was to revoke this guy's license to breathe because he was prematurely ending my life. It was revenge, pure and simple. But when I look back there were other logical reasons to take this guy out. I didn't want any other women to be raped and/or killed or any other police officers to get killed like I thought I had been. One might think this is some kind of post-event rationalization and maybe it is, but it has logic. The question that needs to be asked is, "What would you have done in this situation?" And if you did wait and pass out, figuring you were dying, what would the consequences have been? Would the suspect have killed your partner? Maybe, maybe not. If he had killed your partner he most probably would have escaped to kill and rape again. If I had not pulled the trigger and executed this sonofabitch when I did, there would have been a lot of uncertainty. By pulling the trigger, I ensured the safety of my partner and that of any women this suspect would have come in contact with in the future.

Maybe if I had gone to Homicide with my story there would have been a court case to decide the legality of what I did, but I seriously doubt that I would have wound up anywhere but in the gray bar hotel. And what would happen to Johnny David if I came clean now? There were others to consider besides myself. The DA might go after Ted, even though he had nothing to do with it. I don't doubt that a good attorney might have been able to convince a jury that I had done the only thing I could have done, and could have possibly gotten me off. More likely though, the jury would have tempered a guilty verdict with mercy and I might have been given a light sentence for voluntary manslaughter. I couldn't conceive of a sentence of less than three years, and for what? For a long, very public trial and 10 years of mandatory appeals, appellate court shopping, and legal maneuvers? No, I didn't feel bad. And if the department didn't bring it up again, I sure wasn't going to.

CHAPTER THIRTY-THREE

Gratitude is the memory of the heart
—Jean Baptiste Massieu

April 1982. I stayed in Community Hospital for another three weeks. My voice came back very gradually but never all the way back the way it was before. Now it's just a little gravelly, which isn't too bad. Julianne says it makes me sound sexy. At first I felt like my limbs were made of rubber and my bones were nonexistent. I was very shaky the first time I tried to walk and I needed help, but after a week I could walk without the assistance of other people or any contraptions.

The nurses on all the shifts were friendly and helpful, and I think Julianne was a little jealous. Near 10 p.m. one night, well after visiting hours, there was a knock on my partially open door.

A head peeked around and I saw a woman who looked sort of familiar, but I couldn't quite recognize. When she saw that I was awake, she walked in and introduced herself as Nora Salinski. I immediately remembered she was the last rape victim. I can't say I remembered her face as the one time I had seen it, it was bloody and had a shocked and frightened expression. After an awkward moment, I gestured for her to come in and sit in one of the chairs in the room. She was very pretty, but it looked like she still had a scab or two that were healing on her chin and neck.

We talked for over half an hour. She thanked me a couple of times for saving her life and I tried to deflect those embarrassing words by asking how she was doing. I told her I was most concerned about her mental healing because it must have been such a horrific experience. She told me that the one of the detectives gave her the name of a psychologist who specialized in working with sexual assault victims, and she had been very helpful. Neither one of us mentioned the killing of the rapist or what she saw. She did mention that Sergeant David had suggested she come to see me in the hospital before I went home. He'd told her he thought that would do us both some good.

Nora said that she had moved back in with her parents temporarily. They lived in El Dorado Estates, a nice area of East Long Beach. She said that Ted, Sergeant David, and a couple of the detectives had helped her move her stuff the previous Saturday. Before she left, we promised to keep in touch.

During my hospital stay, other cops were coming in all the time, and some of the friends I had in my neighborhood growing up as well as high school and college buddies dropped in. The Chief of Police and the Deputy Chief of Patrol came by and explained that a committee was looking at whether I should be recommended for the Medal of Valor. The Chief said he was pretty sure I would get it. Since the awards ceremony was in March for the prior year, he said I wouldn't get it until the following year. I told him that was okay with me since I didn't think I should get it just because I got myself shot. He and his Deputy Chief laughed at that and then told me that I had made the department look good at a time when the press was riding our asses about trying to capture the rapist-murderer.

I suppose I could have told the Chief the truth right then and there, but I had a feeling he already knew. He and Sergeant David had worked a patrol car together way back when, and I knew for a fact that the Chief listened to Sergeant David although a lot of others in the top administration of the department didn't like him. Once, I had been on the third floor, walking by the Chief's office, when I heard Sergeant David yell, "What kind of a bullshit policy is that, Chief?" (The Chief had just started a policy of having all of the patrol officers work a ten-and-half hour day instead of just ten, claiming that we couldn't get paid during our half hour code 7 break.) I don't know if it was the complaints from the Police Officers Association or Sergeant David's confrontation with the Chief, but he stopped the policy after two days. Anyway, it wouldn't have surprised me if Sergeant David had told the Chief or at least implied what I had done and what he had done to cover it up.

Morally, I was not concerned about what I had done in dispatching that asshole to his next lower level of existence. I was, however, afraid of what would happen to me if I was found out. In reality, I knew that the world was a much better place with him gone. I think that the Chief, if he knew what had actually happened, felt the same way, and I knew Sergeant David certainly did by his actions to cover me. I don't know if the Chief would have continued to support me if what really happened came out in the press, but since it didn't, I was secure in my job. I felt even better when the Chief told me that I could take as long as I needed to recover from my wounds before getting back to work. (I knew, though, that the City's policy was that if it took more than a year to get back to work, I would be retired. At 31, I wasn't ready for that.)

After I came home from the hospital, it was another eight weeks before I was able to go back to work. There were a couple of times during that period when Julianne and I got a little miffed at each other—from the friction of being together 24 hours a day, seven days a week. After a harsh word or two we would look at each other and laugh. I was happy to be alive and Julianne was very happy I hadn't checked out, and we both realized how lucky we were and how stupid the things were that we were arguing over.

The kids were great and put on a little show for me about good cops and bad robbers. It was complete with costumes that they'd made with the help of their mother and it had me rolling in the aisles. Julianne is a firm believer in the healing power of laughter and she's convinced me of it too. She rented one of the Pink Panther movies and several old Laurel and Hardy tapes. At least three times a week, we watched one of those tapes and I believe they really did speed my healing. They also made me forget the shooting and what I could do about the conflict that was building inside me.

I knew what I did was illegal as all hell, but I didn't think that it was in the least bit morally wrong. And that was my dilemma. I felt the need to justify what I did. Everybody thought I did the right thing but their thoughts were based on the wrong reasons. It was way back then that the seeds of the idea for this book were planted. I never knew if there would come a time when I could tell my story and escape the legal ramifications of my morally justifiable execution of this predator, but I still felt compelled to tell someone.

I couldn't tell Julianne what I had done. It wasn't that I thought she would hate me. I'm sure she would have agreed it was the right thing to do. But she had worked in aerospace in her professional life before becoming a stay-at-home mother and had had no contact with the criminal justice system. I didn't know if I could explain the trouble I would be in if what I did came to some politically leftist or overly ambitious DA She might think that nobody in their right mind would try to push such a case, but I knew that somebody would. The ACLU would have had a field day if it found out that a police officer executed an "alleged" criminal regardless of the circumstances. I would be bait for a media feeding frenzy. My kids would have been harassed and ridiculed in school, and Julianne and I wouldn't be able to show our faces in public. While Julianne is a very smart, strong woman, I didn't think I should load her with the consequences of one of my professional decisions.

But I did know who I could talk to with complete trust and understanding. Ted came over one Saturday just as Julianne and I were leaving to take the kids to a birthday party. I had told Julianne that I would go with her and the kids to the party but when Ted drove up she told me to come by the party when Ted had gone. Ted and I went back into the house and I went to the refrigerator and brought two beers to the living room. After a little small talk regarding my recovering health and Ted's new rookie trainee (the training sergeant asked Ted to train while I was off), I looked at him in silence for a minute and then finally said, "Do you know what really happened that night?"

Ted knew what I meant without me having to elaborate. He said, "No, but I realized some of the evidence was moved around between the time I found you and when the Homicide dicks arrived. I know Sergeant David had a long talk with the rape victim. I know he wouldn't screw you so I never said anything to anybody. You want to talk about it now?"

"Yeah," I said. Then I laid the whole thing out to him. I had never shared with anyone else before that I thought I was dying that night, but I told him. And I said that I was pretty sure I wouldn't have killed the sonofabitch if I wasn't convinced I was dying or I hadn't been shot at all. I told him how the darkness was closing in on me, and my thoughts about my family and my kids growing up without their father. I told him how pissed off I was that I was going to die and this sonofabitch was going to live. I knew I had to kill him before I checked out. I told Ted the flat out truth that I had executed the cutthroat predator and that I was not the least bit sorry. And I told him that right after I stumbled forward and squeezed the trigger into this execrable, whining, miserable piece of shit, everything went black.

When I woke up weeks later and realized I was still alive, I thought at first that if anyone knew, I would be spending the rest of my life in the gray bar hotel. I wasn't concerned what anybody would think of me; I figured 9 out of 10 cops would have done the same thing I did in similar circumstances. Then Sergeant David had come to visit when no one else was around and told me what he thought I had done and what he had done to cover for me.

Ted asked what the Homicide dicks had asked me and I told him about me not being able to talk and how we had communicated. I told him that I thought that maybe Sergeant David had hinted around or that they had half an idea what had happened and weren't real circumspect in their questioning. At any rate, with the eyewitness account and the evidence coinciding nicely, they wrapped up the case. They might have had suspicions, but if they did, they probably figured justice was done regardless of anything else.

When I was done, Ted asked me if I was sure I didn't feel at all guilty for "snuffing out that miserable prick," and I told him absolutely not. If the detectives had asked me the right questions, I would have told them the truth, but since they didn't ask, I wasn't going to volunteer the information. Ted asked why I had told him.

I said, "You're my partner and I had to tell someone. I couldn't tell Julianne. And Ted, as big an asshole as you are, I know I can trust you."

Ted nodded, was quiet for a minute, then smiled and said, "I'll never tell anyone about this. But if you ever make Chief of Police, I'll be Deputy Chief within a week with all the shit I've got on you now." We both started laughing. Ted confirmed my feelings that most cops would have done the same thing. Then he started updating me on what had been going on in the department while I was away.

CHAPTER THIRTY-FOUR

*The only thing necessary for the triumph of evil
is for good men to do nothing*
—John Stuart Mill

May 1982. A few of weeks before my recovery was complete, I started walking in my neighborhood. First, I went just a couple of blocks but I increased the length a little each day. It became increasingly difficult because I lived at the top of a hill. Starting out was easy because it was downhill. The last 200 yards were uphill and I was well winded by the time I got home. The last week before I went back to work, I was able to walk for an hour and a half, but I was hot and sweaty when I returned home, not just from the exertion but from the heat. It was late spring and it was in the high 80s.

One day, I had taken off my shirt and was standing in my garage looking for a pair of needle nose pliers to pull a small stone out of the tread of my hiking boot. It was mildly irritating during that last half mile of my walk when the stone was clicking on the pavement with every step.

My son, who was only three-and-a-half at that time, heard me in the garage and came out to watch. My daughter and my mother-in-law were still in the house reading Dr. Seuss. The garage door was open to the street. Mark and I were standing in the shadows next to my toolbox. My house faces due east and it was around noon. The sun was so bright that day it actually hurt my eyes to look out into the street from our shadowed shelter.

Despite that, something across the street caught my attention. Four male teenagers of high school age were walking up the hill. Two of the teens were tall and the other two were short. This was an odd sight for a couple of reasons. First, the hill they had to climb was steep, and my street, Santa Blas, ended in a cul-de-sac. There was another street, Avenida Valdez, about 30 yards before the cul-de-sac that went back downhill, but the thought occurred to me that if they were going to some house on that street, why didn't they take the shortest route on such a hot day? The other thing that entered my mind was the fact that this was not a holiday and they should have been in school. Even so, I probably would have just figured they were ditching if one of them had not looked over into my open garage and said, "Hey, look at that," and started to cross the street as if to come check out my garage.

As it happened, my neighbor across the street had taken my car to his gas station to change the oil and Julianne had her car at work, so to the casual observer it looked like someone had forgotten and left the garage open while they were off shopping or at work. When this kid reached the middle of the street, Mark jumped at a lizard he saw run out of the corner. The kid saw this movement, turned slightly, and went back to his friends who had continued walking up the sidewalk. This caused me to think that they were up to no good and were probably out looking to commit some daytime residential burglaries. The four delinquents, as I now thought of them, continued walking up Santa Blas then turned and walked down Avenida Valdez. I watched their backs as they went downhill out of my sight.

At that point, I grabbed Mark's hand and said, "Let's go see what these miscreants and malefactors are up to." (I was trying to give Mark a vocabulary by using big words when we talked and then explaining them to him when he asked.)

"What are misafucters, Daddy?" Mark asked.

Suppressing a grin at his more than appropriate malaprop, I looked down. "Bad guys, Mark," I said. "They're bad guys."

Mark and I walked across the street to the corner of Santa Blas and Valdez and looked down. At first, I didn't see any of the suspects. Then, on the right side of the street, I saw one of the tall kids walk to the sidewalk from a driveway closely followed by one of the short teens. Then they continued down the hill. Not seeing the other Mutt and Jeff pair, I bent down to Mark and told him to stay right where he was. I debated taking him back to the house and leaving him with my mother-in-law while I picked up my small .380 caliber pocket gun, but I thought I would just see what the delinquents were breaking into and call the sheriff after I got an address. I had walked downhill by four houses when I saw the other kids standing near a tree next to a driveway. One saw me at the same time and I heard him as he turned to his pal, and said, "They're not home, we better go," and started walking down the street toward his other two companions.

The tall guy apparently hadn't heard his shorter cohort. I walked a little farther and saw that he was on the front porch of a house. He had a small screwdriver in his right hand and was attempting to pry off a screen on the window next to the front door. I walked up the driveway and was almost at the front porch when the kid caught my movement out of the corner of his eye. In one quick motion, he put the small screwdriver in his pocket, stood straight up, and started walking toward the street. I blocked his line of escape and asked him what he was doing. "I was just seeing if my friend Jake was home," he said, and he tried to go around me. I pushed him into the wall of the porch with my left hand and reached into his pocket with my right, pulling out the screwdriver.

"Nobody named Jake lives here and I saw you trying to break into this place by prying the window screen off," I said as I held up his small screwdriver.

"Well it's a house that looks just like this one. Maybe I'm on the wrong street. And I was just fixing the screen. It was loose," spewed the liar. And then he tried to push past me again. I looked around and there was no one around but this burglar and me. I told him that I wanted to see some ID and the kid tried to push me out of the way and get by me again. This irritated me. Since there were no witnesses around, I pushed him against the wall, backhanded him, and told him to knock off the bullshit. I grabbed him by the arm and had started walking him back to the street when his three buddies came into view, coming back up the street.

The fight would have been on at that point except I also noticed Mark had walked down and was only 20 feet uphill from us. I told the group that I knew they were committing burglaries and I had already called the sheriff, which was a lie, but I thought could buy a little time to get between Mark and the crooks. The tall teen who had returned had a big buck knife in a sheath on his belt. He started to pull it from its holder and I tried to grab it but missed. The tall jerk pulled on the sheath and started to open it.

He looked at me and then at Mark. I felt a cold trickle of sweat run down my spine. I was uphill from the young hoodlums and at that time I put my hands out to my side, started backing up, and told them again, "Okay, I already called the sheriff and deputies are on the way." As I started backing up toward Mark, the hoods turned downhill and started walking away.

As they did this I turned and ran, picking Mark up as I did. I ran home as fast as I could. When I got there, I set Mark down next to his sister and grandma, raced to my bedroom closet, grabbed my .45 and Police ID, and ran back down the hill. Halfway down, to my utter amazement, was a sheriff's car and a deputy with the four would-be burglars spread eagle on his hood. I showed my badge and ID'd myself as I approached him. I put my .45 into my waistband and told the deputy what I had seen. He told me that he had a call from a citizen on the next block who had seen the four thugs coming out of his next door neighbor's house.

The incident had frightened me, not because of any danger I felt for myself, but because I had put my son in harm's way. The tall knife-wielding thug made some smartass remark when I told the deputy about him pulling the knife, and I grabbed him and slammed him on the hood of the sheriff's car. The sheriff pulled me off. He handcuffed each of them to each other with two pairs of handcuffs, tall to short. The deputy told me to calm down, and got my information and what I had witnessed. Another deputy arrived and they drove off with the wanna be thugs.

I, of course, know a lot of cops. Some will not get involved in anything when they are off duty. Others will only get involved if a major felony is committed in their presence. But, with my family history of law enforcement, I had kind of an "old school" attitude regarding crime. When my Dad was on LAPD, he was required to carry his gun off duty and to get involved if he witnessed a crime being committed. I think that one of the reasons that the crime rate escalated so much during the '60s, '70s, and '80s was that no one, off duty cops or law abiding citizens, was telling these crooks to knock that crap off when they were doing the little things. Either through fear or thinking it wasn't worth it to get involved, the thugs were never pulled up for minor antisocial behavior, and I think that emboldened them to do more and worse things.

To me, it's similar to parents who let their kids throw fits in stores or let them run things in the home without ever punishing them. The parents are really doing them a disservice because when the kid starts doing that at school or when they get older, they have never had the experience of being told "no." And when a kid grows up and tries to get his or her way in a bar or at a ball game, other people are going to take exception to that spoiled kid's antics and he (or she) will be knocked on his or her ass or worse.

I also tended to get involved because I generally despised two things, for which there is no excuse: stealing and taking illegal drugs. I never did do those things. I've been in supermarkets and seen people steal things and told a checker or a manager, or when the thief wanted to fight, I've obliged him. I was in a movie theater once when the kid in front of me lit up a joint. I gently tapped him on the side of the head, grabbed the joint, threw it on the floor, and stepped on it.

These burglars taught me a valuable lesson, though. If you see a crime being committed when you are with a member of your family, just back away and call the cops. It's not worth risking the life of a loved one. If I'm alone, however, I do feel I have an obligation to make an arrest or at least display my displeasure. I think that if more cops and citizens did that, it would have a significant positive effect against crime.

CHAPTER THIRTY-FIVE

*I think everyone should experience defeat at least once
during their career. You learn a lot from it*
—Lou Holtz

September 1982. I was going back to work the following
week. I wondered if the killing would have any effect on the way
I worked, and I wondered if I would be more tentative in taking
action or less circumspect before I took appropriate action. I was
pretty sure I would be all right. As it turned out, I had nothing to
worry about.

When I went back to work a week later, things pretty much
went back to normal. My first day back several of the cops on
my Watch told me what a good job I did offing that murderous
cutthroat baby-killing predator. By this time I was pretty much
inured to these well-meaning but insensitive remarks. They didn't

bother me at all. I grew up in a police family and was aware of the true meaning of self-defense and that killing was not necessarily murder, but something distinct and different and often justifiable. Some cops, though, grew up in families that were very religious or overly moralistic and when they killed some righteously-deserving dirtbag, their consciences went into overdrive and it started to eat them up inside. Combine an active conscience with post-traumatic stress and you'd get a police officer going off the deep end. He would either commit suicide or become so ineffective or obviously impaired that the department would have to give him retirement.

A couple months after I returned, the Chief retired and we got a new chief, James Cox, from within our own ranks. I didn't know him but I had heard both good and bad things about him. Later, he looked awfully good considering the chief that followed him. I felt he screwed with me more than a little on my promotion to sergeant, but he more than made up for that by appointing me to the sergeant's opening in Vice.

Two months into Chief Cox's administration, the department announced they were going to give a sergeant's test, which they hadn't given in about three-and-a-half years. Ted and I both signed up to take it. Neither one of us really hit the books too hard. Other cops formed study groups and went in together and bought all the books on the reading list. I had two books from the last test. Ted had one I didn't have and I bought a used study guide for one of the other books that just had questions and answers for each chapter. That helped me a lot because it had all the correct answers marked.

On the day of the written test, the Civil Service people escorted us in and sat us at preassigned tables. I was seated next to Jaime Nuestra with whom I had been carrying on a friendly, career-long feud since we were both in the Academy together. When Jaime loudly proclaimed that he was surprised that I had enough grey matter to find my way to the testing room, I just smiled and told him that I really didn't care how I did on this test as long as I ended up just one number higher on the list than him.

After the test was over and Civil Service collected our papers, Jaime and I walked out together. Ted, who had been at a table closer to the door, was waiting for us. When we reached him, Ted said, "C." Jaime and I looked at each other and then back at Ted and simultaneously said, "What?"

Ted repeated, "C. On any question that I didn't know the answer I marked C. Last time I marked B and only got a 62. We'll see if C gets me a higher grade this time." We all laughed.

I was pretty confident because I always did well on tests, even ones I didn't study too hard for. Ted said he knew he hadn't passed it, and Jaime said he thought he had a 50-50 chance. The Civil Service people told us that the test results would come out in four weeks. Jaime and I bet 10 bucks on which of us would finish higher on the list.

***

The first list that came out just included officers who had passed with 70 or above and their scores. I was right at 69 but when the protest questions (questions that were found to be ambiguous) were thrown out I moved up to a score of 72, which put me and Jaime at a tie.

Ted didn't make the cut which made him happy because he didn't have to worry about the oral exam or the departmental evaluation.

I didn't worry too much about either of the next phases of the test. I have always been able to express myself easily and my sergeant and lieutenant both liked me and the work I did. My commander at that time, Walcott, was a jerk and wasn't part of my fan club. He'd overheard me badmouthing him as a kinky-haired Peeping Tom for some of his off duty activities in East Long Beach. He lived in Belmont Shore and always rode his bicycle around at strange hours. He was often seen in the area of Peeping Tom calls either shortly before or shortly after the call came in. Most cops don't believe in coincidence and neither did I. My mistake was to voice my opinion within earshot of that backstabbing rat bastard. But Sergeant David and Lieutenant Kanter would be able to counter his input even though Commander Walcott had his lips so tight on the Chief of Police's ass that he was nicknamed Commander Hemorrhoid.

When the list came out, I wound up number 20. Jaime came out number 23. The higher ups in the department were initially speculating that they would promote 30 to 35 people to sergeants off the list. Then the City came out with their budget that showed a $10 million shortfall (it just so happened that the Police Officers Association and the Firefighters Associations were in negotiations for a three-year contract—funny how the budget shortfalls occurred like clockwork every three years), so it was speculated that the department might only promote 20, which, of course put me right on the bubble. This was not a problem for me. Either I would make sergeant on this list or I wouldn't. I had a good partner, a good beat, and good days off.

A boot sergeant only made $150 more a month to start than I did as a top step patrolman, so if I didn't make it, it wouldn't have broken my heart. If I did make it, I would probably start out on graveyard patrol, a shift I definitely had a hard time with.

But what happened got my hackles up and caused me to fight to make the list. The department promoted the first 17 cops off the list to sergeant in the order in which they finished.

Then the Chief of Police came out with a new policy for the rest of the people on the list. Commander Walcott told the Chief that, as Chief of Police, Civil Service had given him the ability to choose between the top three candidates on any promotional list. The city was now debating whether to extend that power to choose between the top five candidates or completely do away with the policy. Walcott told the Chief that if he didn't exercise that power the city would take it away. Walcott talked the Chief into believing that the officers at the bottom of the list were inferior in quality and so it wouldn't make any difference to skip a cop at the bottom of the list for one lower if the lower officer had more education or some other quality that the department might be able to use. Walcott convinced the Chief that the best thing to do was to give the next three officers on the list an additional non-civil service oral exam.

Thirteen months after the first sergeant was promoted from the list, the top three candidates left on the list were ordered to take another oral exam. Mike Tinker and Rob Bottoms, both with 20 years on the job, and I were ordered to take this non-civil service oral exam in front of the two Deputy Chiefs. Both Chiefs were decent guys so, while I didn't think taking another oral was equitable, I thought I would get a fair shake.

I was the third officer to take the exam following the order in which we wound up on the list. It was a low-stress question-and-answer type exam with the emphasis on current and possible future crime problems in the City of Long Beach. I thought I did all right, but I wasn't surprised or disappointed when the Chief made Tinker and Bottoms sergeants in each of the following months. There were still six months left before the list expired and I was number one now, so I was pretty confident that I would make it soon. Then the Chief came out with another policy change.

The next three people on the list would have to take another non-civil service oral exam. By this time I was getting a little hot. Why was I going to have to be the only officer to take three orals (two of them non-civil service) to get promoted? I talked to Karl Mundst, the President of the Long Beach Police Officers Association, and he told me that the way the Civil Service code was written, the Chief was within his legal rights. He also told me that he had heard that Commander Walcott had a lot of influence with the Chief and that I would probably be made the test case to prove that the "rule of three" could be implemented by chiefs.

That was exactly what happened. The third oral exam lasted an hour and forty minutes and was conducted by three commanders, Walcott, Pirelli, and Hutchinson. Walcott, I've already mentioned. Hutchinson wasn't too bad a guy for a commander although he was a little impressed with himself. But Pirelli, who had just made commander, had a reputation for being a crook.

When we had a scandal at our police pistol range and a sergeant was fired for misappropriating funds, Pirelli was the lieutenant. When he was in charge of the Police Academy he charged the rookies each a dollar a week for the Trustees who mowed the lawns and acted as janitor and caretakers. I found out later that there was a "Trustee Fund" but it was operated from the jail at the downtown police station and Pirelli was pocketing the money and taking the staff out for drinks on Friday nights.

Anyway, they kept giving me scenarios of possible misconduct by officers and then would ask me what I would do. In every situation, one of the things I said I would do was to contact the officer to get his side of the story. After the third such answer, Walcott jumped on me and told me that I was too close to the officers and that I would be reluctant to discipline them.

I told him that wasn't true, but I felt it was important to get both sides of the story before determining if there actually was misconduct. Hutchinson nodded his head in agreement, but Pirelli jumped all over me, reiterating Walcott's argument that I was too close to the troops. It got to be such a high stress oral that

I was hot, sweaty, and defensive. Anything I said was attacked and vilified by Walcott and Pirelli. Hutchinson didn't say much after the first four or five attacks on my answers, but at least he wasn't trying to bury me. At any rate, I was so pissed off after this onslaught that I stopped at the Reef Restaurant and had two double martinis at the bar.

Although I was ultimately promoted to sergeant, I wasn't sure it was worth it.

CHAPTER THIRTY-SIX

You get out of life what you put into it.
I think you need a bit of luck but you also make a bit of luck.
I think that if you're a pretty decent person
you'll get back what you put in

—John Key

January 1984. In our police department, when a new sergeant is made, he or she is usually given one of the less desirable jobs: the Front Desk, the Booking Desk, Jail Sergeant, or Communications. I was sent to Communications on Watch 3. I was told by several of the sergeants who had worked Communications to be careful because some of the dispatchers, most of whom were women, could get kind of catty and there was some animosity between a few of them.

I had always had a lot of respect for all of the dispatchers. They were well trained, and could pull a patrol officer's ass out of the fire more often than not. Also, a lot of them developed a sixth sense and seemed to know when a call looked like a set up. Often they would remember calls of locations where violent offenders lived or where weapons had been used in the past.

I worked in Communications for 14 months and actually enjoyed my time. All of the dispatchers were great. Some were better than others but it looked to me that the better ones were the ones with the most experience, meaning the others would only improve. All of them displayed great senses of humor. The banter was loud, raucous, profane, and continuous. I'm sure that in today's world we would all be fired for sexual harassment, verbal harassment, obscene gestures, and general conduct unbecoming police officers or police personnel.

But we did one hell of a job. Actually, they did one hell of a job. When I started in Communications, I really didn't know anything. The senior dispatcher, Barbara, tutored me along until I was able to pretend that I was supervising a group of people who needed little or no supervision. The dispatchers kept calm and businesslike during vehicle pursuits, officer involved shootings, officer needs help calls, crimes occurring now, setting up perimeters, and other high stress situations. Most of the time, they knew where the units were and directed them to places where they were needed. When they didn't know where the units were it was usually the officers' fault and not the dispatchers.

I was fortunate that there were no major officer deaths or riots while I was in Communications. Later in my career, I listened to them while dispatching during these situations and they have always been professional and calm, and the concern and compassion can be heard in their words and voices. Furthermore, the stress and frustration that cops feel on the streets affects the dispatchers just as much. As businesslike as they are when dispatching, I've seen some of them shed tears or physically shake after having to send officers to make a death notification to parents of a small child or put out a dispatch about one of our officers dying in a traffic accident.

***

On rare occasions, it appears as if I have fallen into a vat of feces, but I suddenly come out smelling like night blooming jasmine. After a new list for sergeant came out, I was going to be replaced in Communications. As was usually the case, I would be going to Patrol.

My lieutenant came and told me that the only Patrol Sergeant's opening was for graveyard patrol with Mondays, Tuesdays, and Wednesdays off. I could never sleep more than a couple of hours during the day and was always tired when I worked that shift. I had a hard enough time trying to stay awake on the graveyard shift when I had a partner. Working alone as a graveyard sergeant was going to be tough. I was going to have to see if there was some way I could get an IV filled with coffee to keep me awake during my shift.

Then a good and merciful God intervened on my behalf. The sergeant in the Homicide detail was making lieutenant. The sergeant in Robbery was being moved to Homicide. The Deputy Chief of Detectives wanted to make my buddy, Chip Maranaro, the Robbery sergeant, but Chip didn't want it. Chip loved where he was in Forgery/Fraud and maintained that the best detectives were there. He told me that handling a real estate fraud case was 10 times more difficult than your average homicide who-done-it. As a result of perfect timing or Divine Intervention, none of the other detective sergeants wanted to leave their units and none of the patrol sergeants who had seniority on me wanted to give up their 4/40 work week, with three days off every week, to work five days a week in Detectives.

So I became the new Robbery sergeant.

Since I was new to the unit, I sat in on the interrogation of a robber who had held up a couple of fast food restaurants. Tom Baker briefed me before we brought the suspect to one of our interrogation rooms. He went over all the evidence he had: witness statements, suspect's fingerprints on the counter at one place and on the door jamb at another, and the weapon the patrol officers found in the bushes near where the suspect was arrested. After reviewing all of the evidence, we took the suspect to the interrogation room.

This turned out to be a classic suspect interview with the bad guy lying and denying at first. Tom did a masterful job getting the suspect, Jeremiah Wood, to tell us a bogus account of how he just happened to be in the areas of the robberies, but hadn't been to either fast food joints. Tom then had him write out his false account of what happened. Tom read it, made a few corrections of spelling errors, then had Jeremiah initial the corrections and sign and date the paper.

Jeremiah Wood was now locked into his lies. That's when Baker pulled the rug out from under him. "Jeremiah," Tom said, "you're fucked. Your written statement is full of so much bullshit it could fill a cattle car. You wrote that you had never been at Taco Bell or Der Wienerschnitzel. We have your fingerprints on the inside door frame of Taco Bell and on the counter of Der Wienerschnitzel. You said you never had a gun and don't know how it got in the bushes where you were arrested, but we have three eyewitnesses that will swear in court that they saw you throw that .38 into the bushes. We have seven witnesses at Taco Bell who saw you point that gun at the girl behind the counter and rob her, and two who will testify to seeing you rob the Der Wienerschnitzel. If you tell us the truth now, the DA and the courts will go a lot easier on you. Why don't you do yourself a favor and tell us the truth?"

At that point, Mr. Wood gave us a full confession. I was impressed by Tom's interrogation and learned a lot from him.

CHAPTER THIRTY-SEVEN

"It is better to be divided by truth than to be united in error.
It is better to stand alone with the truth,
than to be wrong with a multitude
—Adrian Rogers

October 1987. At the start of this tale, I implied that Truth brings the light of day on whatever subject it shines. That light doesn't always illuminate things that are pretty. In fact, quite often it shows some very ugly things. Regardless of the ugliness exposed, there is the satisfaction in finding the Truth. And Truth can only be found after examining both sides, sometimes all sides, in complicated conditions, situations, incidents, and occurrences.

The very essence of police work is finding the Truth. I would hope that it is clear that I revere and respect the Truth. If I didn't, I wouldn't have the dilemma I'm in now and you wouldn't be reading about it. As I grew up, my mother and father taught my sister and me that the highest virtue was honesty and the foundation of honesty was Truth. If we misbehaved, we would get in trouble, but if we lied about it, we were in bigger trouble and the consequences were much greater.

I learned the importance of Truth at a young age. I practiced what I had learned in school and at home, even when I could have escaped punishment and/or embarrassment by telling a small lie. I avoided the temptation to lie with one glaring exception when I was 16. I had met a beautiful young lady, Maggie, who was working at a hamburger stand in Inglewood. She gave me her phone number and I called her that night and made a date to take her to a movie the following Friday. I asked my dad if I could use the family car, a 1964 Chevy station wagon, for the date. Dad asked me where I was going (we lived by the Los Angeles Airport, in Westchester, at that time). I told him I was taking this girl to a movie up in Hollywood. He told me that Hollywood was a cesspool and I couldn't go up there. So I promised that I wouldn't.

When I picked Maggie up, she looked so good that I decided to impress her by driving up to Hollywood and seeing a movie at the Pantages Theater on an exclusive engagement. We had a great time and I was going to ask her out again, but that didn't work out. The next day my dad asked me where I had gone with my date. I told him I took her to the Paradise Theater in Westchester. He asked me if I had gone to Hollywood for pizza. When I told him "no," he produced the parking stub where I had parked the car to go to the movies in Hollywood. I hemmed and hawed for a minute before my dad said, "Let's talk about this out in the garage."

I knew that in addition to all of my dad's tools, the garage also housed my dad's heavy punching bag and speed bag. I was sure that when we walked through the door to the garage, I was going to be dad's focus bag for the next few minutes. Even though my father had only spanked me once or twice as a child, I feared the worst. I knew I had lied to my dad, I knew I was wrong, and I was ready to accept my punishment, although I certainly wasn't looking forward to it. My dad was 6'3" and weighed a good 210 pounds. When we walked into the garage, my dad surprised me by telling me to sit down. I opened a lawn chair and sat while he sat down at the small desk he had out there. I had half expected a backhand, or for the old man to pick me up and yell at me while he held me off the ground, but that didn't happen.

In a quiet voice, my dad told me that he was grounding me for a month. Then the knockout punch came. Not a physical punch, but a verbal one. With his rock-steady glare, he said, "You don't know how disappointed I am that my son is such a piece of shit that he could look me right in the eye and lie to me. You're grounded for a month. Go on. Get out of my sight."

I would have rathered he used me for a punching bag. I tried to apologize, but I think I was choking back tears. Dad just waved me off and I went back to the house. This man had been my hero for as long as I could remember and now he thought I was a "lying piece of shit." Like all teens, I had rebelled a little at parental restrictions, but I still had the utmost respect for both of my parents. That talk with my father had a life-changing effect on me. From that point on, I vowed never to lie again and I never did. I may have unknowingly screwed up facts, but I never intentionally lied, except later to suspects in the furtherance of justice or to my wife if she asked me if the dress she was wearing made her look fat. Because in all other instances I was scrupulously honest, I occasionally got into trouble because of telling the Truth.

I have always found that telling the Truth was the right thing to do. In a practical sense, it is always easier to remember the Truth than a lie. It was my personal belief that whatever the consequences of telling the Truth, it was still better than the feeling I had walking out of that garage after my dad's talk.

CHAPTER THIRTY-EIGHT

Honesty is more than not lying.
It is truth telling, truth speaking, truth living, and truth loving
—James E. Faust

July 1988. One day, I was called into the acting lieutenant's office. Phil Becker was one of the smartest guys on the department. He had been the Homicide Sergeant for years and when the Crimes Against Persons lieutenant had suddenly retired, the Chief of Police had taken the Chief of Detectives recommendation and appointed Phil to temporarily fill the position until a new lieutenant was promoted. Phil was very competent, efficient, and well respected. Unfortunately, he was also a no bullshit, opinionated cop who didn't hesitate to tell the brass when, where, and why some of their harebrained ideas or policies were wrong, idiotic, and/or counterproductive. That probably explained why he was never promoted to lieutenant, commander, or deputy chief.

When I sat down in his office, Phil told me that the department was starting a new unit, Gang Detectives, and that they needed a sergeant to lead it. He asked if I would be interested. At that particular time in the early 1990s, gangs were running rampant in Long Beach and all of California. Confronting the gang problem would be the cutting edge of law enforcement in the city and state. I accepted.

Before I could even get started, I was involuntarily transferred to Vice. There had been four sergeants in Vice: one was the Administration Sergeant, who handled scheduling, ABC (Alcohol Beverage Control) permits for bars and restaurants, bingo inspections, and complaints; one worked in the field on nights, one worked in the field on days, and one alternated between nights and days, depending on demand.

The need for Vice sergeants had suddenly risen abruptly. One Vice Sergeant had made lieutenant; another decided to retire suddenly after 34 years on the job, the last 15 in Vice; a third had been injured on duty when he was stabbed in the ribs with a short knife while arresting a street prostitute; another, Phil Banks, who had three years seniority on me, had put in his transfer after working Vice as a detective. Since no one else wanted to go to Vice, and I had the lowest seniority in Detectives, I was put in the Sergeant's position that alternated between working nights and days. I wound up doing the job of two sergeants and supervising eight detectives, sometimes on two different shifts.

Even though my transfer was not what I wanted, my new lieutenant, Roland Ballard, told me that it was an honor, in a way. Vice and Narcotics, although part of the Detective Bureau, constituted the Special Investigation Division (SID). The Chief of Police had to approve any detective, sergeant, or lieutenant going into SID. There was a logical reason for this. Most people, including many in law enforcement, see many vice and narcotic violations as victimless crimes. Any law enforcement agency is vulnerable to corruption. Those that seek to cause that corruption look for the easiest point of attack. In most agencies that weak point is in Vice and/or Narcotics. There is so much money in illegal drugs, gambling, and prostitution that the temptation for a less than straight arrow cop is obvious.

The Truth got me into some minor trouble when working Vice. The Deputy Chief of Detectives contacted me after I was working the day shift for a month. A woman reporter from the Long Beach Press-Telegram, Kay Schmitz, was going to write a story about street prostitution along Pacific Coast Highway and Anaheim Streets. The Deputy Chief told me to take her out and show her the hookers and explain to her how we were addressing the problem.

Kay Schmitz came into the Vice office and introduced herself. I took one of our undercover cars and we headed eastbound. I pointed out the streetwalkers I saw. From Daisy Avenue to Cherry we saw nine of them on either side of the street. Kay said, "Really? Most of those girls are pretty homely."

I told her, "Oh yeah, Long Beach has to have the ugliest hookers in the world. I don't see how they make enough money to buy food, let alone feed the drug habit they almost all have."

I had so little experience interacting with the press that I didn't realize that I should have added, "That's off the record." A week later, when the Press-Telegram printed the story, I was called into the office of the Deputy Chief of Detectives. When I walked into his office, he handed me a copy of the paper. He had considerately highlighted my quoted comment in yellow. "Did you say that?"

I looked at the yellow-marked quote about our city's ugly working girls that was attributed to "Vice Sergeant Edward One."

Then, I glanced up sheepishly at the Deputy Chief and said, "Ah, yes." He started berating me, telling me that what I said was unprofessional and put the department in a bad light. I told him that my only defense was that what I said was "God's Truth."

He continued to harangue me for another couple of minutes until I got a little piqued myself and stopped the Chief by saying, "Wait a minute. What's wrong, Chief? Did the Chamber of Commerce call and tell you that companies are canceling conventions here because I said we had ugly hookers?" At that, the Deputy Chief just shook his head and said, "Go on. Get out of my office."

Sometimes the Truth will set you free. Other times, it will kick you in the seat of your pants.

CHAPTER THIRTY-NINE

No matter how educated, talented, rich or cool you believe you are,
how you treat people ultimately tells all....
—Unknown

August 1989. I wound up working Vice for four and a half years. Being both a day and night sergeant worked well with my family schedule. With both my son, Mark, and daughter, Margie, in sports at school, I could work either days or nights as their games came up. With Margie's soccer and softball, and Mark's football, basketball, and baseball, my flexible schedule allowed me to see almost all of their games.

Toward the end of my tour in Vice, the Chief of Police retired and the search for a new chief started. The Chief who had retired wasn't a bad chief. When he'd started, he had faced some resistance, since he was our first Black chief. He'd also changed our pursuit policy about chasing suspect vehicles that sped away when the cops tried to stop them in marked police cars with their lights flashing and sirens blaring. The prior policy was that if a car fled, the officers could go in pursuit. Now, a supervisor had to okay the pursuit, and he would only do that if the car was wanted for a felony or posed an immediate threat to life and property. This caused more than a little discontent with the patrol officers. The fact was that there were a lot of injuries to cops, citizens, and suspects because of these pursuits. Also, there might have been a thumping or two of those who refused to stop, once the pursuits were over. In retrospect, our policy needed to be revised.

I may not have liked all the changes the Chief made, but he was the Chief and I realized that he was looking at a bigger picture than I saw looking out of my patrol car. He made a couple of other unpopular decisions, but they seemed to stop when he forced an old captain, who had been his chief advisor, to retire. After that happened, the Chief seemed to grow in his position and was starting to look like a pretty good guy. Then he announced that he was retiring. I wished he would have stayed for another five years.

The city manager had only been in his job for a little over a year when he started looking for a new chief. He interviewed our three Deputy Chiefs, and two of our Commanders. The city manager then opened up the position to command officers from outside agencies. He wound up choosing a Deputy Chief from San Francisco PD. Big mistake. You know you're in trouble when every section of the department starts getting calls from SFPD saying things like, "He's your asshole, now," or "Thanks for moving our hemorrhoid to your city."

At first, the new chief seemed all right to the street cops and detectives. We heard some grumblings from some of the command staff and a lieutenant or two, but their complaints didn't seem to affect us, at least not right away. One of the first things the new chief did was put a three-year limit on the time detectives could work in Vice or Narcotics. I knew the arguments for switching guys out of those two units, but I didn't agree with them.

I loved working Vice. We always dressed casually because we were undercover every day. In addition, it was good for your ego. If one sex didn't find you attractive on a particular day, the other did. I hated to leave it, but my three-year limit was up. At that time, I was told that there were no detective sergeant jobs open so I would have to go back to Patrol and lose my detective pay. That was the bad news. The good news was that I was given the choice of whatever shift on Patrol I wanted. Since my wife was working part time and Margie and Mark were still in school and sports, I decided Watch 2 day shifts were my best option. The hours were 7:30 a.m. to 5:30 p.m., and my days off were going to be Thursday, Friday, and Saturday.

When I got back to Patrol, I soon realized two things: first, the new chief may have come from San Francisco PD, but he was originally from Hell. And, second, being a good sergeant is twice as hard as being a good police officer. I became aware of what a jerk the new chief was from his policies and his discretionary appointments and promotions. I found out how hard it was to be a good sergeant when I discovered how difficult it was to keep my fellow officers and myself out of trouble because of the new policies enacted by the chief.

I'd started thinking the new Chief of Police was a crook when he appointed one of our lieutenants to commander and in less than two months made him a deputy chief. I knew this lieutenant, Gerald Brusino, was a crook from the time I worked in Vice because two of the bookies we arrested were connected with him. With a warrant we had, we'd rammed the door of a house the bookie was renting to make book. He didn't live in the house, but used it as his office. After we caught him while he was trying to get rid of his "pay and owe sheets," he started yipping that we were wasting our time because "Jerry B will take care of this."

Another time, the bookie we arrested had an address book that had J. B. on the inside flap on the line marked "in case of emergency," and had Brusino's home and office phone numbers.

But the most convincing proof was from one of our Vice guys who got a call from the LAPD Organized Crime office at the LA Airport. It seems that the LA detectives at the airport saw a well-known Mafia hood get off a plane from Philadelphia, rent a car, and drive to Curley's restaurant in Signal Hill with two of their detectives following him. (Signal Hill is a small city completely surrounded by Long Beach). This hoodlum was meeting with a big male White guy in a suit, but the LA dicks didn't know who he was and asked our Vice detective and his partner to see if they could go into Curley's and identify the man the hoodlum was meeting with.

When our Vice undercover guy walked into Curley's, he made the hood from the description given to him and saw the crook hand an envelope to the big White guy in the suit, who he immediately recognized as our very own Lt. Gerald Brusino. The crooked lieutenant then placed the envelope in his inside suit jacket pocket.

Our Vice officer then went outside and told the LAPD detectives who the Mafioso had met with and about the delivery and acceptance of the envelope. He went back to the station, told the Vice Lieutenant and SID commander, and all three of them went into the Chief of Police's office and told him. The Chief called Lt. Brusino's secretary and left a message for the lieutenant to report to the Chief's office ASAP.

A half hour later, when Brusino arrived, the Chief asked him about the mobster and the envelope handoff at Curley's. With a look of astonishment on the lying sack of shit's face, Brusino pulled the envelope out of his suit pocket and said that he didn't know the guy was an organized crime figure. He only knew him as a gem dealer. He told the Chief that he bought some small uncut diamonds from the alleged mob guy and was planning on selling them to some of our downtown jewelers. He opened the envelope and showed the uncut stones to the Chief.

The fact that no one had seen Brusino give the mafia guy any money, check, or other remuneration was explained by the lieutenant as having paid for the diamonds previously. The Chief then had one of his commanders do an investigation, but he was unable to prove anything criminal. Because of the cloud over his head, Brusino, who had 28 years on the Department, told the Chief that he would put in his retirement papers, effective in six months, rather than face discipline. The Chief accepted this. Unfortunately, the Chief suddenly retired a month later, and the crooked bastard pulled his retirement papers. Then, within a couple of months, the new Chief of Police made him a commander and then a deputy chief. This corruption scandal was not well known in the Department, but certainly the Chief who was retiring had told the incoming Chief. Why would an honest Chief appoint a deputy chief who was strongly suspected of having organized crime connections? Why, indeed.

CHAPTER FORTY

A man's dyhing is more the survivors' affair than his own
—Thomas Mann

February 1994. I worked as the Day Patrol sergeant in North Long Beach for almost three years. We had no major incidents during that period. During one of my shifts in North Long Beach, Communications advised me to call my old partner, Ted Norris, at home. When I called Ted, he told me that he just heard that our former Sergeant, Johnny David, was in a hospital in Huntington Beach. Ted told me that Johnny had some type of respiratory problem. It wasn't supposed to be too serious, but he was going to be in the hospital for three or four days for tests and observation. Ted, who was working Sex Crimes at the time, told me he was off on Friday and we should go see Johnny then. This was a

Wednesday and I was also off Friday, so we agreed I would pick Ted up about 10 a.m. and we would go see Johnny at the hospital. Ted said he would call him Friday morning to see if we could save him from a hospital lunch by sneaking him in some fast food.

Ted had moved back to East Long Beach about half a block from his parents' house. When I pulled up in his driveway at about 9:30 a.m. and beeped my horn for Ted, he came out his front door a minute later. He had a somber look on his face and his eyes were red.

Ted, who was so shitty at giving death notifications, looked me in the eyes and softly told me that when he called to see if Johnny wanted a hamburger or some tacos, Johnny's daughter answered his cell phone and told Ted that Johnny had passed away an hour earlier of an embolism that went from his lung to his heart.

Neither one of us said anything for a few minutes. I was thinking of all the times Johnny had pulled our fat out of the fire or we waylaid him with one of our pranks. I'm sure Ted was thinking similar thoughts. Finally, I shook off my memories and said, "Hop in, Ted. We're going to Tracy's to have a drink or two in Johnny's honor." Tracy's was a bar that was owned by one of our larger-than-life retired sergeants. After the first couple of drinks, I called Julianne and told her about Johnny passing away and not to wait dinner for me. She said she understood and, choking a little bit, told me I should not drive home as she knew I would be blitzed.

Ted and I laughed and drank and told Johnny David stories and drank and cried and drank and repeated the cycle. About midnight, one of the waitresses called the station. I don't know how she did it, but she somehow got one of the undercover Vice units to pick us up and take us home. The two Vice cops, nicknamed "the Beak and the Butterball" because of their most prominent physical attributes, had been working street hookers that night, and as part of their ruse they were appropriately driving a limo that Narcotics had seized through the asset seizure statute.

When they arrived at Tracy's, the Beak was dressed in the uniform of a chauffeur and the Butterball was wearing the most garish plaid tuxedo I have ever seen. Both Vice cops had to assist us off-duty comrades in arms, who were still alternating their moods between the maudlin and the hilarious, to the back door of the limo. With some difficulty, Beak and Butterball poured us into the back. There was a small bar in the back of the limo, and Butterball laughed the whole way to Ted's house, which was only about 10 blocks away, as he watched our attempts to pour ourselves a couple of road drinks. This, of course, was an exercise in futility.

Somehow they were able to get us to Ted's front door, lean us against the posts on the porch, and ring the doorbell. With Jeanne's help they were able to drag me to the couch and lay me down. Ted had passed out while leaning against the post and. With Beak at his feet and Butterball grabbing under his arms they were able to maneuver him into the house, place him in his La-Z-Boy, and recline him. That was the position we were still in when Jeanne woke us the next morning with cups of strong coffee.

I was hungover, had a headache, and my mouth tasted like what I thought a well-used cat box would taste like. Jeanne told us that she had sent the kids around the corner to their grandparents' house. She then asked us if she could make us some breakfast of scramble eggs and chicken livers, which we both vigorously declined. Did I mention that Jeanne could be downright mean at times? When Jeanne went to get us some more coffee, I told Ted that he was not a very good host. I told him that a good host would have done what the Eskimos were rumored to do and let me sleep with his wife. Jeanne heard this from the kitchen and yelled, "If you think I would have slept with either of you smelly drunken slobs last night, you're nuckin' futs. You guys were sweating booze and, as a matter of fact, you still smell like it."

After a couple of cups of coffee, Ted drove me to my car parked in the rear of Tracy's. I drove home and spent the rest of the day piddling around recovering from my hangover. My wife Julianne told me how upset she was with Johnny's passing. Like most women, she saw him as funny and charming. He always treated women in the most gentlemanly manner, opening doors and speaking in a much less profane way than when he was talking to cops, at least until he knew the women better. Then Johnny might get a little bawdy, but always in a slightly naughty, humorous way.

Johnny's daughters notified the Department and the POA that his funeral would be a week later. I turned down an overtime job working on my day off on a movie that was being filmed in the city. I couldn't miss Johnny's send-off. I knew he would have done the same for me. The wake afterward was a real celebration of Johnny's life. Nearly all of the coppers who had worked for him the last couple of decades showed up and the stories brought the bittersweet memories and laughter back to all of us.

One of the Homicide dicks told the story of seeing Johnny at Francois's Restaurant once when several of the detectives were out with their wives one Saturday night. Johnny, who was single at the time, walked through the dining room and took a seat at the bar. A very attractive, tall redhead came in a few minutes later and took a seat a couple of stools away from Johnny. They saw him buy the pretty woman a drink and move to the stool next to hers. After about 20 minutes, one of the cops went to the pay phone by the restrooms. He called the restaurant, spoke for a few minutes, and then went back to the table. A couple minutes later, one of the waitresses came into the now crowded bar, looked around, and asked, "Is there a Long Beach police sergeant Johnny David here?"

Johnny turned, stood up, and said, "I'm Sergeant David." The waitress said, "Congratulations. St. Mary's hospital just called and your wife delivered a six pound, ten ounce baby boy." Johnny's protestations that he wasn't married fell on deaf ears as the redhead stalked out of the bar.

At the wake, I was only drinking light beer since the memory of my last week's hangover was still fresh in my mind. As I was passing a table in route to the men's room, a hand reached out and stopped me. I looked down and the hand was attached to a beautiful woman. It took me a minute before I recognized Nora Salinski. She was seated a small table by herself and I immediately took her hand and sat in the chair next to her.

A single tear coursed down her left cheek when she told me that it was good to see me. She asked about my family, and when I asked about hers, she told me that she was married and had two girls, one seven and one five. (Had it been that long ago?) Nora said that Sergeant Johnny David had kept in contact with her. She said that her husband, a dentist, didn't want her to come to Johnny's funeral or wake because he felt it "would pull scabs off of old wounds." When Nora related to him how she couldn't have made it without all of the aid, moral support, and the recommendations of victims' groups and counselors that Johnny had given her, her husband agreed that they should go, but Nora had told him that this was a very personal thing for her, and that she wanted to go by herself.

We talked about her recovery and my recovery. Neither of us mentioned the rape or the sending of The Phantom to his ultimate nether destination. After about 10 minutes, I stood and told Nora that I had to go to the restroom, but not to move, that I would be back in a minute and we could continue our conversation. When I came back, Nora was gone.

CHAPTER FORTY-ONE

Corrupt officials are usually close-mouthed
and open-handed
—Evan Esar

February 2001. After working Day Patrol for almost three years, I realized that I was going to max out on my retirement in two and a half years. I thought it would be good for my retirement to get the extra couple of hundred dollars detective's pay, so I put in for detectives. A sergeant friend of mine, Mike, was transferring to Narcotics from the night Juvenile Sergeant's position. Juvenile was pretty much a low stress job that I thought would ease me into retirement, so I applied and got it.

The following Tuesday afternoon I started in Juvenile. A year earlier, the department had moved the Juvenile Division off the fourth floor of the police building and into a former medical building in the 1900 block of Pacific Ave. I had been given a card to get into the fenced in parking lot at the rear of the building that you had to access from the alley. I was assigned a desk in a large room that I shared with Martin Baylor, who was the School Resource sergeant. Since he worked days and I worked nights, we were only in the office together for couple of hours a day, but we got along great. Although our supervisory philosophies differed somewhat, our personalities and senses of humor meshed perfectly and we had a good time during the hours we shared the office.

As it turned out, I did retire in early December of 2004.

***

The last big event of my career happened on May 1, 2001. Before transferring to Juvenile, I had been picked as one of the supervisors to train with a new special unit that would be activated in the event of civil disorder or natural disasters. It was called the Mobile Field Force. We learned crowd control and disbursement on foot, in riot formations, or in police cars in a coordinated thrust and push method. We were trained in the proper way to shoot bean bags and rubber bullets from shotguns, and the most effective way to lay down tear gas.

When I transferred to night Juvenile, I had to give up my position on the Mobile Field Force. I think it was because they trained during the day and the department didn't want to have to pay me overtime. Anyway, when some anarchists invaded Long Beach that May 1st, I was sorry I wasn't in that unit. They were trained to—and in fact did—send these obnoxious twerps back on their asses.

This is what transpired. At about 0900 hours (9 a.m.) that morning, our Intelligence unit obtained information that a group of organized anarchists were planning to come to Long Beach.

Although this "demonstration" had been well planned in advance by the anarchist/communist leaders, word did not go out to their idiots until that morning. We found out that these anarchist zombies were supposed to bring their backpacks filled with their weapons of choice: rocks, bottles, bags of urine and feces, M80s and cherry bombs, small explosives, etc. Once the office of the Chief of Police was notified, there wasn't much time to set up a response. The Chief gave that job to one of our Commanders, Tom Hambly. Tom had been a street cop for about 10 years before he made sergeant and therefore he responded like a street cop rather than a police administrator, which was a good thing.

Commander Hambly almost immediately set up a command post on Chestnut and Broadway. Then he delegated different tasks to the other commanders and lieutenants who were assigned to the command post and let them loose to do their assignments.

The Mobile Field Force was immediately activated. The Watch 3 officers were called and ordered in at 1230 hours (12:30 p.m.), since our intelligence was that the anarchists were supposed to meet at Lincoln Park between 1330 and 1400 hours (1:30 and 2 p.m.). Watch 2 officers were advised that they would be working late. All traffic officers were ordered to the station and briefed about where and how to set up traffic barriers and where to divert traffic. Most of the detectives were ordered to get into their uniforms. That had to be quite a trick for some of the older, wider ones. Undercover Vice and Narcotics detectives were briefed, and ordered to drift into Lincoln Park and infiltrate the anarchists as they arrived.

The Deputy Chief and Commander in charge of logistics sent officers to gather riot gear, traffic barriers, and less lethal weapons like bean bags and rubber bullets and the shotguns that shoot them. After the preliminaries were in place, Hambly sat down in the mobile command post with all the command staff assigned and mapped out a plan. The advantage to the command post system is that one person, the officer in charge, regardless of rank, has the final say in what the police response is going to be. The negative, is that, in reality, the higher ranking officers will sometimes try to impose their ideas on the officer in charge. A chief will come in and say something like, "I see what you're doing, Commander, but don't you think that might look bad to the press or the public?" An ambitious underling will then ask the Chief what he would do and implement what the Chief suggested.

I heard from my reliable sources that one of the deputy chiefs did attempt to get Commander Hambly to change one of his orders and Hambly turned to him and said, "Are you taking over this command post, Chief?" When the Deputy Chief declined to take responsibility, Hambly told him that he should leave the command post. This Deputy Chief was noted for holding grudges, and Tom had to know that he might get a knife in the back at some later date, but he stuck to his guns and continued to supervise the best police response to an attempted anarchist disruption that I have ever seen or heard of. Tom had even put the City Prosecutor's Office, the DA's office, and the presiding judges on notice so they would be prepared for the large number of arrests that were expected to be in court in the next day or two.

The information we had was that the anarchists wanted to get onto Pine Avenue to break windows and close down restaurants, banks, and businesses on that street as it was the main commercial area in downtown. The traffic units set up manned barricades at Broadway and Pacific, Broadway and Long Beach Boulevard, Ocean and Pine, and 3rd Street and Pine. They stopped northbound traffic from Ocean Boulevard on Pacific and Pine and Long Beach Boulevard, and southbound traffic from 3rd Street on those same streets. Then they equipped the Mobile Field Force with riot gear of helmets, clear shields, extra long batons for those on the front line and the less lethal beanbag and rubber bullet shotguns and tear gas for the squad leaders.

A third of the Mobile Field Force was deployed at Pine and Ocean and a third at 3rd and Pine; the rest stood by in reserve. The traffic units on the east/west streets were assisted by patrol units in riot gear. The Day Juvenile units were ordered into uniform and deployed around the City Hall/Central Library complex. Night Juvenile was ordered in at 1400 hours (2 p.m.), in uniform, and relieved the Day Juvenile Units at 1500 hours (3 p.m.). The Day Juvenile detectives went back to Juvenile and set up to book and process juvenile anarchists when they were brought in.

I was so disappointed that I wasn't still on the Mobile Field Force. They saw a lot of action that day. The anarchists were caught completely off guard at how prepared we were for them. We made over 110 adult arrests, and 70 juvenile arrests.

I was told that the cops who had the most fun were the undercover Vice and Narco guys. The head anarchist was identified early when he tried to penetrate the Mobil Field Force at Pine and Ocean. He would repeatedly rush up to the line of officers blocking Pine. He knew just how far to go to stay out of the reach of the long batons and he would stop just far enough away to keep from getting hit. He would throw small baggies of who knows what at the officers, yell some profanities, and then rush back to the mob of anarchists who were lined up about 10 feet behind him.

On his third rush to the line of riot cops, he was followed by two undercover Vice cops. Before he could turn back to his fellow travelers, the two Vice cops pushed him back toward the riot cops, who proceeded to utilize the long batons for their intended purpose and then arrest him and drag him off to the booking van at Broadway and Pine.

The anarchists became confused when their main leader was arrested. He was apparently going to give some signal that would have started a general barrage of the cops with rocks, bottles, and baggies of urine and feces. When the Mobile Field Force Commander got on the loudspeaker and announced that this was an illegal assembly and that they were ordered to disburse, the anarchists held their ground as they had been instructed by their leaders.

They remained even when they were told that less lethal weapons were being deployed and aimed at them, but some of them started to break for whatever cover they could find when the specialized shotguns were aimed. After the bean bags and rubber bullets were fired, these "demonstrators" did, indeed, disburse. Unfortunately, most of them ran into the Mobile Field Force officers who had been held in reserve. Some of these officers were on Ocean west of Pine and some east of Pine. Other rioters, many of whom had been hit by the bean bags and rubber bullets, were arrested by the Mobile Field Force officers who came out between the front riot line to mop up any remaining rioters.

A similar scene happened at 3rd and Pine when the anarchists refused to comply with the lawful order to disburse there. One of the undercover Narco cops told me that when the squad leaders aimed their less lethal shotguns at that crowd, he had some cover behind a pickup truck with a camper shell, parked at the curb. Some anarchist woman tried to push her way next to him and he pushed her in the street just as the squad leaders fired. The woman was hit in the butt with a bean bag and knocked to the ground. The Narco guy told me that he had never before heard such a vivid and profane description of himself and his ancestry as this woman arose, glared at him, and then limped off, vainly trying to evade arrest.

Commander Hambly and his staff had set up booking and transportation vans at three locations, so the arrests and reports were completed and hung around the necks to each of the arrested anarchists, along with their property in a plastic bag with string.

The vans were then loaded and taken to the Booking Desk or Juvenile respectively. By 1630 hours (4:30 p.m.), we were relieved of our rather boring duty guarding the City Hall/Library Complex. We went back to Juvenile and the Day Juvenile officers went "end of Watch."

The Day Juvenile officers had already completed most of the bookings by the time we got back, but as they were leaving, another van-load came in and we started booking them in. I was processing a tall, scrawny 16-year-old when I noticed a huge swelling on the left side of his lower cheek. I smiled and told him that he had the worst case of mumps I had ever seen. He replied, "Real funny." When I asked him what had happened he said that he had been hit in his cheek when he was trying to duck the bean bags that were shot at his crowd. The beanbags and rubber bullets are usually aimed at the lower extremities, but if the target ducks, sometimes the prey gets hit someplace more sensitive. I told him, "Well, if you anarchists didn't want to listen to lawful orders, you were going to get hit with the consequences. In your case, that was a beanbag to the face." I was laughing as I told him this. I swear this idiot's response was, "Well, we're not coming to Long Beach anymore." He said it like we would be upset that his anarchists wouldn't come back and try to destroy part of our city again. I smiled more broadly and told him. "Good. Now, you understand."

While I was walking up the steps to the front of the station, I saw Lieutenant Jake Rubin. We had worked together a couple of times on Watch 3 Patrol. He always like to remind me, whenever he saw me, about how he had "saved my life" one night in Recreation Park when a suspect van pulled away with my hand caught in the window. Jake had broken the window with his Kel-Lite before I was dragged away.

As I was talking to Jake, who was in full uniform, a group of the anarchists, who were carrying protest signs, started to gather at the foot of the steps. Their leader very meekly approached us and asked if his group could march in front of the police station. Jake told them, "No, go over there," pointing to the sidewalk away from the entrance. They humbly complied. Anarchists, like every other group of cowards, get their courage from large numbers. Alone or in small groups, they're just a bunch of wimps.

I have done things as an individual policeman or with my partner that I am very proud of. I have worked in detective and patrol units that did such good jobs that I could point to them with satisfaction and pride. The first of May in 2001 was the day that I was most proud to be a Long Beach police officer because of the job our department did in turning back the hordes of barbarians calling themselves anarchists. While I don't often see the police brass in action, and therefore seldom give them praise, our Command staff did such an amazing task in anticipating, coordinating, deploying manpower, and meeting the challenge that every other law enforcement agency ought to study what we did and follow our blueprint in addressing these attacks on order in our society. That is the Truth.

***

When I retired in December 2004, my old pal Joe Johnson had already retired. He told me that he had been hired back as a "dinosaur"—a non-career police officer—doing background checks on prospective police officers and firefighters. Joe told me they were looking for two more background investigators, and asked if I was interested. I was. It was a job that paid very well when you were working, but you couldn't work more than 20 hours a week.

I did that for eight months and when all of the backgrounds were done, Joe and I got transferred to storefront police offices.

This was a boring job where we had to man these storefronts to take reports from people who came in occasionally.

I did that for another year. Then, Julianne and I moved to Arizona. We found a house on a hill just outside of Prescott that was perfect for the two of us.

Margie and Mark had both moved out a couple of years before. Margie had finished college and was working as a nurse at St. Mary's in Long Beach. Mark had joined the Marine Corp in 2003. He was sent to Iraq in 2004 and fought in Fallujah. When he returned, he might have stayed in the Corp if he was stationed at Camp Pendleton but he was stationed at Twentynine Palms Marine Base, which the Marines unaffectionately called "Twentynine Stumps" and is in the middle of the Mojave Desert.

After his honorable discharge from the Marine Corp in 2004, Mark got a job as a bartender in San Diego and started taking some classes at a local community college. Both Margie and Mark appeared to be happily single, with no marriage prospects on the horizon.

After we were comfortably ensconced in central Arizona for a couple of years, only returning to SoCal once or twice a year to visit the kids and our other relatives, Margie called in 2005 to announce that she was engaged to a Long Beach firefighter. Having just gotten over that shock, a month later Mark called to tell us he was engaged to a CPA. During the next year, we were able to see both of our kids marry. Knowing the problems a few of our friends have had with some of their kids' spouses, we have been quite fortunate that both our children married well.

By 2014, we had four grandkids. Margie and her husband, Cal, gave us Jason in 2010 and Daniel in 2014. Mark and his lovely wife Rhonda had Carl in 2011 and Rita in 2013. This necessitated us driving the seven hours to California several times a year, but it was worth it every time.

We got involved in the Arizona community and both of us started volunteering with different groups. I joined the Lions Club, where a couple of other retired Long Beach cops were members. I had been an Elk in California and did a transfer over to the Prescott Elks and got on their investigation committee, interviewing new Elks. I also volunteered in the emergency room changing beds at the Yavapai Regional Medical Center once a week. Julianne joined the Lionesses, and started as a driver for People Who Care, taking the elderly and infirm who could not drive to their appointments.

The first Christmas season we were in Prescott, we were told to go to Acker Night. All of the businesses around the Courthouse Plaza stay open, and individuals and groups of musicians play all kinds of music in these businesses. At the Hassyampa Hotel, the local Sweet Adeline group, The Song of the Pines, were singing. After hearing them, Julianne told me, "I really like that group. I got one of their pamphlets. I'm going to try out for them." I told her that I had heard her singing in the shower and she couldn't carry a tune in a bucket.

A month later, she came in one night after what I thought was a night out with her new girlfriends and proudly told me, "Well, I passed my audition and I am now a Sweet Adeline." Amazed, I looked at her and said, "Are they changing their names to the Sour Susannas?" She threw me a looked that would have petrified a lesser man.

In late October of 2018, a series of bad events happened. First, our health took a temporary (but draining) turn for the worst. I caught pneumonia and was down, basically bedridden, for three weeks. Just as I was getting better, Julianne came down with a respiratory illness that our doctor said was near pneumonia.

While I was nursing Julianne, as she had done for me, I got a text message from Ted. Nora Salinski, the rape survivor, had passed away from lung cancer. This seemed almost inexplicable to Nora's husband because Nora had never smoked.

Ted sent me the information about Nora's funeral and celebration of life, but I explained our health problems to him and asked that he tell Nora's husband why we were unable to attend. I told Ted how terrible I felt about not being there, but he told me to try not to worry about it.

In the last week of December, after missing Christmas with our kids and grandkids, the worst news came. Julianne and I were both finally feeling back to normal. We decided to uplift our spirits by Watching "It's a Mad, Mad, Mad, Mad World" on one of the cable movie channels. We were laughing ourselves silly during the scene where Jonathan Winters tears up a gas station and beats up the two owners when my cell phone rang in its charger in the kitchen. I had stopped laughing by the time I answered it, thank God.

It was Jeanne Norris and I could tell by the tremor in her voice that something was terribly wrong. At first, I thought something must have happened to one of their five kids. Jeanne, trying to keep herself together, choked a little, then told me that Ted had passed away that morning. She told me that they were drinking coffee on their backyard patio when Ted just slumped in his seat. Jeanne whacked him in his arm thinking he was joking but he really wasn't responding. She shook him and then grabbed her phone and dialed 911.

The fire station was right around the corner from the house they had purchased a couple of years before when they moved back to Long Beach. Paramedics arrived in less than five minutes and immediately de-fibbbed Ted and started CPR, put him on a gurney, got him into the ambulance, and took him to Community Hospital. Ted didn't respond. The Emergency Room Doctor told Jeanne that he thought Ted had the "widow maker" heart attack.

I couldn't think of any words that would alleviate her pain, so I just told her how sorry I was and that Ted was a good man and the best partner I had ever had. I gave Julianne the phone and they commiserated for a while as I sat in stunned silence, remembering all Ted and I had been through. When Julianne got off the phone, she told me that Jeanne would call in a day or two when she had made all of the funeral arrangements.

I didn't sleep much that night. I was tossing and turning and thinking about all of the crazy stuff Ted and I had been involved in. I finally got up, went to my liquor cabinet, and poured myself my former partner's standby drink, Irish Creme and vodka. He always said it tasted just the same as Irish Creme, but it got you to the Emerald Isle twice as fast. I don't know why he drank it. I don't even think he was even part Irish, although he might have been part Russian, which would explain the vodka. At any rate, I made the drink, sat in my easy chair, raised the glass and said, "Here's to you, Ted. The best partner I ever had." I downed the drink and a short while later dropped off into an uneasy sleep, dreaming about driving around in a squad car with that crazy bastard next to me explaining why it was my fault that we were getting all of the crappy calls.

A week later, Julianne and I drove out to Long Beach for Ted's funeral and wake. It was so sad seeing Jeanne and his kids sitting in the front row with Ted's parents and his brother and sisters. The wake was a bittersweet affair. I remember talking and laughing about all of our escapades with a bunch of the retired and soon-to-be retired cops we worked with. Looking back on it now, the memory of the drive out there, the funeral, the wake, and the drive back to Arizona is viewed through a misty fog. More than any other man, Ted was my brother, and now he was gone.

EPILOGUE

Ye shall know the truth, and the truth shall make you free
—Bible, John 8:32

January 2020. With Johnny David, Nora Salinski, and Ted all gone, there was no one else who knew the Truth of my execution killing of the serial rapist/murderer known as The Phantom. Even though no one else now alive knew what had really happened, I still did, and it was a burden. It was not the heavy burden of guilt, because I never felt any guilt. It was not the burden of facing an injustice because I felt that the ultimate justice had been meted out. It was a burden of a Truth left untold. I had an uncontrollable need to release myself of that.

In the year and half since Ted died, I have been writing this and it really has released me from this weight. I can tell this story now without getting anyone else in legal jeopardy. Whatever anyone thinks of what Johnny David, Ted Norris, and Nora Salinski did, none of them will face a jail term for covering up my actions. I don't know if any magazine, internet, or book publisher will ever publish this; I didn't write it for that purpose.

I sent a copy of this book to the Los Angeles County District Attorney's Office and the California Attorney General's Office. There is no statute of limitation on murder, so I don't know what they will do with this case that is almost 30 years old and has no witnesses. If some ambitious prosecutor wants to make a name for himself and waste the taxpayer's money, let him try. I'm right here in Prescott, Arizona. Come and get me.